How to Get
SAVED
and Know It

How to Get Saved and Know It
© 2012 by Alfred Stevens

Published by Insight International
4739 E. 91st Street, Suite 210
Tulsa, OK 74137
918-493-1718

All Scripture quotations are taken from the Holy Bible: King James Version.

ISBN: 978-1-890900-70-0

Library of Congress catalog card number: 2012930456

Printed in the United States of America

CONTENTS

PREFACE

I, Alfred Stevens, was saved in 1964.

I had been carrying a gospel tract for years. I had it memorized (can quote it even to this day) but, the tract never did a thing for me. Then, one day an incident in my life led me to thinking, "There's got to be more to life than this."

Through a friend's friend, I made an appointment to meet with the pastor of a main-line denominational church. The pastor and I sat in his office on opposite sides of his desk. He kept showing me scriptures; reading some, and having me read some. After each, he would ask me, "Do you believe that?" I would say "no" to some, "I don't know" to some, and then he hit on one that I said "yes" to. I started crying; I knew there was a definite change in my life – I felt so free. The pastor did not enlarge on the scripture that saved me; he didn't say anything about the Holy Spirit, speaking in tongues, or anything; but he did kind of take me under his wing.

That same evening, I threw away my cigarettes, quit drinking, and quit cursing. Even though I knew nothing about tithing, the Holy Spirit must have impressed it upon me to tithe. I started tithing immediately, putting my tithe in the Sunday School offering. Finally after two or three Sunday services, I caught on and put my tithe in the morning service offering.

I started witnessing to everyone, not knowing a whole lot of what I was talking about. I thought one believed for salvation with his physical heart. I'd check the newspaper and if there was a religious service taking place in the area, I was there; especially after I heard about the baptism with the Holy Spirit. It wasn't until about twenty years later that I spoke in tongues. I could have spoken in tongues immediately upon salvation had someone told me I was indwelt by the Holy Spirit.

Shortly after salvation, I accepted almost every job in the church that was offered to me: Sunday School teacher, greeter, leader of Saturday men's prayer meeting, head of young boys' program, and sometimes leading prayer in church services. The only offices I turned down were Sunday School Superintendent (wife's ex was still living), and that of an elder (did not speak in tongues). Later in life, I drove several Sunday School buses and vans.

During the last ten years or so, I have seldom attended church – I just felt it was a waste of time. I still had a desire for a closer relationship with God, but I felt like I could be more selective and receive more from Christian books and TV programs. In fact, it was through the ministry of an Oklahoma rancher on TV, that I became acquainted with the differences between Law and Grace, and with salvation by believing on the Cross and what Jesus did for us on that Cross.

One night the Lord called me to preach the above paragraph. I was 78 years of age, had never preached or even spoken before an audience, and preaching was the last thing on my mind. I knew the above was vastly different from that which was being preached and taught out there, and would be an offence to practically everyone, especially to pastors. After realizing none would allow me to use their pulpit, especially after telling them what I would be preaching, I decided I would start in my living room and let the Lord take care of future meeting places. I would awake in the middle of the night and preach to myself for several hours.

One night the Lord said, "We're going to write a book; it will be faster in reaching the people. Time is of the essence; people are dying and going to Hell, not knowing what all I did for them on the Cross." Just as preaching was the farthest thing from my mind; so, also, was the thought of writing such a book. But how can one say "no" to a God Who sent His Son, Jesus, to die that we might have life everlasting. Here's the book!

Chapter 1

THE HOLY BIBLE

The Bible is the story of the creation, fall, and redemption of man. It is the inspired or revealed Word of God, written by men of God, as they were moved upon by the Holy Spirit of God.

Genesis 1:1 "In the beginning God created the heaven and the earth."

God is a Trinity; three Persons in One: God the Father, God the Son, and God the Holy Spirit. God has always existed, exists now, and will exist for all eternity.

The attributes of God are as follows:

1. God is Holy; He is the Supreme Holy Being, the Deity.
2. God is Sovereign. He is absolute.
3. God is Self-existent; no beginning; no end.
4. God is Infinite. He is without end; without limit.

5. God is Omniscient. He is all-knowing; past, present and future.

6. God is Omnipotent. He is all-powerful.

7. God is Omnipresent. He is everywhere; always present.

8. God is Love.

9. God is Grace.

About 6000 years ago God made the first man, Adam, in His own image, after His likeness. Man is spirit and soul living in a body. The body dies, but the spirit and soul live forever. Why did God create man? We are objects of God's love. He wants us to love Him and fellowship with Him. That's why He made man with an attribute of will; to choose to respond to God's love or to reject it.

God gave Adam one commandment. Adam disobeyed, constituting sin, and when he sinned, he died spiritually, losing communion and fellowship with God, his Creator. Immediately, his soul (mind, will and emotions) took on the sin nature, a rebellious attitude toward God. And because all mankind are children of Adam, we have inherited the sin nature. Sin separated man from God.

Romans 3:23 *"For all have sinned and come short of the Glory of God."*

Romans 6:23 *"For the wages* (penalty) *of sin is death* (eternal separation from God)*; but the gift of God is eternal life through Jesus Christ our Lord."*

Hebrews 9:22b *"...without shedding of blood is no remission* (of sin)*."*

***Romans 5:8* "*But God commendeth his love toward us, in that, while we were yet sinners, Christ died for us.*"**

As soon as Adam sinned (God foreknew that man would sin), God put His plan in motion whereby man's sins could be forgiven and man could be brought back into fellowship with God.

God has provided various means for the sins of the people to be covered, looking forward to the ultimate sacrifice of the Cross. Mostly, the means was faith plus an animal sacrifice. During Christ's earthly ministry, they were to adhere to the Law of Moses plus repentance and water baptism. The exception to the above would be Abraham who believed that God was able to perform what He had told him and his faith was counted to him for righteousness (right standing with God). Today, after the Cross, all we have to do to be saved and to be reconciled to God is believe that Jesus was the Son of God, came in the flesh, shed His blood for our redemption from sin, died on the Cross in our stead, was buried, and rose the third day.

As soon as the sinner believes this with all his heart, he is saved and immediately God sends the Holy Spirit to indwell him to help him live his life in Christ. From that moment on, he is in Christ for all eternity.

Now, the flip side of man's eternal fate. There are two spirits in the world; the Holy Spirit and Satan, the devil. As long as you're on this earth, you are serving one or the other. If you reject Jesus and what He did for you on the Cross; instead of spending eternity with Jesus, you will spend eternity with Satan in the Lake of Fire.

Why would anyone want to spend eternity in the lake of fire, when they can spend eternity with Jesus Christ. In the lake of fire, there is darkness, weeping, wailing, and the gnashing of teeth. The worm dieth not, and the fire is never quenched. Those who go there will forever be thinking, "Why didn't I accept the free salvation Jesus provided on the Cross when I had the chance and rejected it?" "The worm dieth not" means bad memories will never be blotted out and all your earthly passions and lusts will be magnified and will never again come to fruition in all eternity. Don't let a few minutes of pleasure in this life keep you from going to Heaven. It is like one drop of pleasure (Hell) compared to an ocean of bliss (Heaven).

See Chapter "HOW WE ARE SAVED TODAY".

Chapter 2

FAITH AND BELIEF

I'm going to write this chapter as if FAITH and BELIEF are synonymous. I don't think we will get into too much trouble if we look at them as if they have the same meaning.

I know a man who describes faith as "taking God at His Word". Now let's go to the Bible and see what It says about faith.

Hebrews 11:1 *"Now faith is the substance of things hoped for, the evidence of things not seen."*

Hebrews 11:6 *"But without faith it is impossible to please Him* (God).*"*

Romans 1:17b *"...The just shall live by faith."*

Romans 10:37 *"So then faith cometh by hearing, and hearing by the Word of God."*

The above scriptures are pretty explicit; if we're going to receive anything from God, we're going to have to have faith.

I Corinthians 1:18a "For the preaching of the Cross is to them that perish foolishness;..."

I Corinthians 2:14 "But the natural man receiveth not the things of the Spirit of God: for they are foolishness unto him: neither can he know them, because they are spiritually discerned."

II Corinthians 4:3,4 "But if our gospel be hid, it is hid to them that are lost: In whom the god of this world hath blinded the minds of them which believe not, lest the light of the glorious gospel of Christ, who is the image of God, should shine unto them."

You might ask, "How can a man receive salvation when it is presented to him?" He doesn't have faith because he doesn't understand the Bible; he doesn't understand because he doesn't have the Holy Spirit to enlighten the Word to him; and then his mind is blinded by the devil. Without faith, it is impossible to please God.

Romans 12:3b "...but to think soberly, according as God hath dealt to every man the measure of faith."

I Corinthians 3:5 "Who then is Paul, and who is Apollos, but ministers by whom ye believed, even as the Lord gave to every man?"

The above question is answered in these two verses. God gives to every man the measure of faith to get saved; to believe on what Jesus accomplished on the Cross for salvation. This faith is a genuine opening of the heart, and we can without any reservation say: I know that Jesus Christ is the Son of God. I know that He died my death. I know that He shed His blood for the remission of my sin. I know that He rose from the dead, and that He had power to overcome sin and Satan. The Holy Spirit not only woos the individual into pursuing salvation, but He also removes the blinders from the man's mind that he may have a receptive heart for salvation. The Lord makes it so easy that anyone can come to salvation: all they have to do is believe (with the faith given them) the Gospel; not of works, lest any man should boast.

I believe most people in Christendom today think "faith" is thrown about loosely and given freely by God for whatever they need faith for. But, according to the first four scripture verses in this Chapter; after salvation, to receive anything from God, you're going to have to have faith; so do a lot of digging in the Word; of course, with the help of the Holy Spirit, Who, after salvation now indwells you. I've heard that one must hear something seven or more times before they really hear it and get it down in their heart. Just keep plugging and faith will come for that which you are wanting to receive.

Now, a few words concerning BELIEF.

> BELIEVE: Persuaded, totally and fully persuaded beyond a shadow of a doubt; know sincerely, really certainly, surely, genuinely, with heart and soul; without doubt; know that you know.

Until you believe it (what Christ did on the Cross), you can't have it (salvation). The sinner must first realize that he is a sinner (Romans 3:23), that the wages for sin is death (Romans 6:23), that he is in need of a Saviour, and that God has provided that Saviour by sending His Son, Jesus Christ to die on the Cross. Christ died our death, shed His blood for the remission of our sin, and rose the third day. When we believe that the things Jesus accomplished on the Cross for us certainly, truly, and surely happened, we are saved; declared righteous and brought back to fellowship with God.

To receive salvation or any other thing from God, we're going to have to believe. The Scripture is sometimes inadequate when saying in what or in Whom we are to believe. When It says to believe in Jesus, are we to believe in the Jesus in the Old Testament; the Jesus Who was born in Bethlehem; the Jesus Who was the Son of God; the Jesus Who walked the streets of Jerusalem for three years, teaching, preaching, healing, and performing miracles; or the Jesus Who suffered and died on the Cross, Who shed His blood for the remission of our sins, and Who was buried and rose again the third day.

James 2:19 "Thou believest that there is one God; thou doest well: the devils also believe and tremble."

It is imperative that we be very careful what we believe.

Galatians 3:7 "Know ye therefore that they which are of faith, the same are the children of Abraham."

Abraham received eternal life simply by believing what God told him. It was counted to him for righteousness. Now we gain eternal life simply by believing what Christ did on the Cross; not by works, lest any man should boast.

Just believe the Gospel (not a gospel, but the Gospel) for salvation. If you really believe, God will save you.

I'm not talking about a mental acknowledgment or a "repeat after me" salvation, or saying the "sinner's prayer". I'm talking about a genuine, heart felt, Holy Spirit driven belief that your eternal destiny is based on what Jesus did for you on the Cross.

Romans 1:16 "For I am not ashamed of the gospel of Christ: for it (the Gospel; not our works, a denomination, nor anything that we can do, but rather The Gospel) **is the power of God unto salvation to everyone that believeth; to the Jew first, and also to the Greek."**

It <u>does not</u> say it is the power of God unto salvation to everyone that repents, and is baptized, joins the church, gives 10% of their income, does good works, and believes.

These things may be alright after salvation, but so far as our salvation is concerned, it's based totally upon our faith in the Gospel of Christ and what God has said concerning the finished work of the Cross.

When Mary Magdalene saw Jesus after He was risen, she told the disciples (the eleven) that he was alive and they <u>believed not</u>. Jesus appeared to two disciples: they told the remainder of the disciples and they <u>believed not</u>. Afterwards, Jesus appeared unto the eleven and upbraided them for their <u>unbelief</u> and <u>hardness of heart</u>.

Matthew 9:20-22 Woman with issue of blood twelve years received healing because of faith.

Matthew 8:5-13 Centurian's servant was healed of palsy: as the Centurian believed, Jesus did.

Matthew 15:22-28 Woman's daughter was vexed with a devil. She worshipped Jesus and said, even the dogs eat the crumbs that fall from the Master's table. The daughter was made whole that same hour.

The Jews had nothing to do with Gentiles; in fact, called them dogs. Jesus did also in Matthew 15:26. But, by their faith in the healing power of Jesus, the above three Gentiles received healing.

On the other hand, Jesus was always reprimanding the Nation of Israel and the twelve because of their unbelief, or of their little faith.

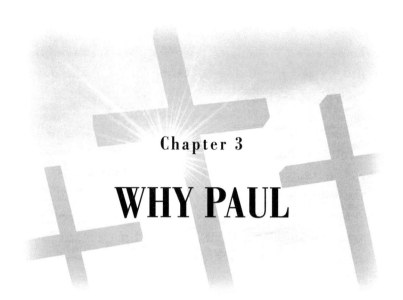

Chapter 3

WHY PAUL

Acts 9:15 ***"But the Lord said unto him*** (Ananias, a Jewish disciple at Damascus)***, Go thy way: for he*** (Saul of Tarsus) ***is a chosen vessel unto me, to bear my name before the Gentiles, and kings, and the children of Israel."***

Ananias layed hands on Saul and he was filled with the Holy Ghost. Immediately, Saul began preaching Christ in the synagogues, that He is the Son of God.

Acts 20:24 ***"But none of these things move me, neither count I my life dear unto myself, so that I might finish my course with joy, and the ministry, which I have received of the Lord Jesus, to testify the gospel of the grace of God."***

Saul's (now Paul's) whole ministry was to proclaim the Gospel of the Grace of God.

Galatians 1:11,12b ***"But I certify you, brethren, that the gospel which was preached of me is not after man. For I***

neither received it of man, neither was I taught it, (by man) *but by the revelation of Jesus Christ.*" (the ascended Lord of Glory)

Paul had received this revelation during a three-year period in Arabia with just him and the Lord. If Paul received everything that he is preaching and writing from the Lord Jesus Christ, where is Christ at the time of all this revelation? Well, He's in Heaven. He's in Glory. After His resurrection, we hear so much of our preaching and our Sunday School material from the four Gospels, which is not wrong to a degree. But that all took place before the Work of the Cross. After the Work of the Cross was accomplished, Jesus ascended back to Glory, and the Lord Jesus Christ is now going to tell this man, Paul, what to tell the whole world, not just the Gentiles and Jews, but all the world.

Romans 11:13a "For I speak to you Gentiles, inasmuch as I am the apostle of the Gentiles..."

Ephesians 3:2 "If ye have heard of the dispensation of the grace of God which is given me to you-ward:" The you-ward is speaking of Gentiles.

Galatians 1:16a "To reveal his Son in me, that I might preach him among the brethren;..." (Gentiles)

That's Paul's specific calling; to take this Gospel of Grace to the Gentile world. This is almost a total reverse of the Old Testament. There, God was dealing only with the Jew, but a few Gentiles picked up some of the gleanings. But now, the message of Paul is going primarily to the Gentiles; but there are a few Jews that come into the Body of Christ.

As the Law was given to Moses on Mt. Sinai for Israel, the doctrines of Grace for us were given to Paul, at Mt. Sinai.

Galatians 1:16b,17a *"...immediately I conferred not with flesh and blood: Neither went I up to Jerusalem to them which were apostles before me; but I went unto Arabia,..."* (that would be Mt. Sinai)

Common sense should have told Paul to go to Jerusalem and look up Peter, James, and John, and the rest of the twelve whom he knew had walked with Jesus for three years, but the Gospel God wanted Paul to preach was entirely different from that which Peter and the eleven preached. Therefore, Paul went directly into Arabia where the Lord Jesus Christ revealed to him the Gospel which he was to preach.

Galatians 1:18 *"Then after three years I went up to Jerusalem to see Peter,* (Paul went to share with Peter some of the new revelations he had received, but Peter never did get them all. He never could comprehend all these revelations that the Apostle Paul had received) *and abode with him fifteen days."*

In Acts, Chapter 13, Paul exhorted the Jews in the synagogue at Antioch. He reminded them how God had brought the people out of Egypt, how He suffered their manners for forty years in the wilderness, how He gave them judges, prophets, and kings, and of David's seed, God raised unto Israel a Saviour, Jesus. The Jews at Jerusalem, and their rulers did not know who Jesus was, and as a result they fulfilled the words of the prophets when they condemned Him. Though they found no cause of death in Jesus, yet desired they Pilate that He should be slain. And when they had fulfilled all that was written of Him, they took Him down from the tree, and laid Him in a sepulcher. But God raised Him from the dead. God hath fulfilled unto us (their children), the promise made to the Fathers, in that He hath raised up Jesus again, now no more to return to corruption. Be it known unto you therefore, men and brethren, that through this man (Jesus) is preached unto you the forgiveness of sin. And by Him all that believe are justified from all things, from which ye could not be justified by the law of Moses.

Acts 13:46 *"Then Paul and Barnabas waxed bold and said, It was necessary that the word of God should first have been spoken to you* (Jews), *but seeing ye put it from you, and judge yourselves unworthy of everlasting life, lo, we turn to the Gentiles."*

Acts 13:47 *"For so hath the Lord commanded us, saying, I have set thee to be a light of the Gentiles, that thou shouldest be for salvation unto the ends of the earth."*

Acts 15: There was contention between Paul and Barnabas and some apostles and elders in Jerusalem about the new believers needing to be circumcised and to keep the law of Moses in order to be saved. Peter said, why tempt ye God, to put a yoke upon the neck of the disciples, which neither our fathers nor we were able to bear? It was concluded that the new believers would do well if they abstained from meats offered to idols, and from blood, and from things strangled, and from fornication.

Acts 20:24 Paul is determined to keep his joy and finish his ministry, which he received of the Lord Jesus, to testify the gospel of the Grace of God.

Acts 20:26-28 Paul says, I am pure from the blood of all men, for I have not shunned to declare unto you all the counsel of God. He admonished elders to feed the church of God which He (Jesus) hath purchased with His own blood.

Acts 26:16 When Paul was converted, Jesus said He was going to make him a minister of these things which he had seen, and of those things in the which I will appear unto thee.

Acts 26:18 "To open their eyes, and to turn them from darkness to light, and from the power of Satan unto God, that they may receive forgiveness of sins, and inheritance among them which were sanctified by faith that is in Me."

Acts 26:20 Paul preached first at Damascus, Jerusalem, coasts of Judaea; then to Gentiles: repent, turn to God, and do works meet for repentance (way of salvation then).

Acts 26:23 Paul preached later that Christ should suffer, and that He would be the first to rise from the dead, and should show light unto the people, and to the Gentiles.

Acts 28:28 Paul says, The salvation of God is sent unto the Gentiles, and they will hear it.

Galatians 2:7 Paul says, the gospel of uncircumcision was committed unto me, as the gospel of the circumcision was unto Peter.

Galatians 2:9 After 14 years when Paul went to Jerusalem; Peter, James, and John gave to Paul and Barnabas the right hands of fellowship; that Paul should go to the heathen and they to the circumcision.

Galatians 2:16 Paul says to Peter: **"Knowing that a man is not justified by works of the law, but by the faith of Jesus Christ, even we have believed in Jesus Christ, that we might be justified by the faith of Christ, and not by the works of the law: for by the works of the law no flesh shall be justified."**

Galatians 2:20 **"I am crucified with Christ: nevertheless I live; yet not I, but Christ liveth in me: and the life which I now live in the flesh I live by the faith of the Son of God who loved me and gave Himself for me."**

Galatians 2:21b **"...If righteousness come by the law, then Christ is dead in vain."**

In Chapters 3, 4, and 5 of his letter to the Galatians, Paul is saying some of them were foolish in that they were returning to works of the flesh (law) instead of living by faith.

Galatians 3:6,7 **"Even as Abraham believed God and it was accounted to him for righteousness, Know ye therefore that they which are of faith, the same are the children of Abraham."**

Galatians 3:10 **"For as many as are of the works of the law are under the curse: for it is written, Cursed is every one that continueth not in all things which are written in the book of the law to do them."**

Galatians 3:11 **"But that no man is justified by the law in the sight of God, it is evident: for, The just shall live by faith."**

Galatians 3:13,14 "Christ has redeemed us from the curse of the law, being made a curse for us: for it is written, Cursed is every one that hangeth on a tree: That the blessing of Abraham might come on the Gentiles through Jesus Christ; that we might receive the promise of the Spirit through faith."

Galatians 3:26 "For ye are all the children of God by faith in Christ Jesus,"

Galatians 5:16 "Walk in the Spirit, and ye shall not fulfil the lust of the flesh."

Galatians 5:18 "But if ye be led of the Spirit, ye are not under the law."

Galatians 5:24 "And they that are Christ's have crucified (put to death) *the flesh with the affections and lusts."*

I Corinthians 15:10 "But by the grace of God I am what I am; and His grace which was bestowed upon me was not in vain, but I labored more abundantly than they all, yet not I, but the grace of God which was with me."

II Corinthians 11:23-28 Paul was warning the Corinthians concerning false preachers and how he was more a minister of Christ than they. Also the following afflictions: 39 stripes (five times), beaten with rods (three times), stoned, left for dead, preached the next day (one time), shipwrecked (three times), in the deep (one night and one day), in journeyings often, in perils of waters, robbers, mine own countrymen, heathen; in the city, in the wilderness, in the sea, among false brethren; in weariness, painfulness, watchings, hunger, thirst, fastings, cold, and naked-ness; and the care of the church daily.

II Corinthians 12:7-9 Paul was also given a thorn in the flesh, the messenger of Satan to buffet him, lest he should be exalted above measure. Paul besought the Lord thrice that it might depart from him. The Lord said, My grace is sufficient for thee; for my strength is made perfect in weakness.

WHY PAUL? Not because we think he was the greatest apostle who ever lived, or because he wrote some one-third of our New Testament, or because he established more Christian churches than anyone; but, because the Lord Jesus Christ personally saved Paul and called him to preach salvation to the Gentiles (us), today, in the Age of Grace, by the Gospel of the Grace of God; which Gospel was revealed to no one before it was revealed to Paul. It is Paul's Gospel by which we are saved today. There is no other way.

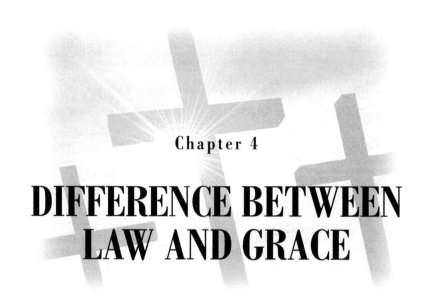

Chapter 4

DIFFERENCE BETWEEN LAW AND GRACE

A dispensation is a period of time during which God laid particular dispensational instructions to the human race. When God called Moses and the Nation of Israel out of Egypt, He brought them around Mt. Sinai. God called Moses up into the mountain. What did He give to Moses? Law. And Law was a dispensation. It was a dispensation to the Nation of Israel; God's demands upon the Nation as to how they were to worship and how they were to live. The law was in three parts. It was first and foremost the Moral Law, the Ten Commandments. It was the Ritual Law; how to worship, and how to approach God with the sacrifices, priesthood, etc. Then it also had the Civil Law; how to deal with your neighbor and how to settle disputes, etc. The Cross ended the Law. Jesus said in Matthew, "I am not come to destroy the Law, but to fulfill it."

Ephesians 3:2 *"If ye have beard of the dispensation of the grace of God which is given me to you-ward* (to Gentiles).*"*

This is in total opposition to law and is now dispensed by Paul.

I Corinthians 4:1 "Let a man so account of us, as of the ministers of Christ, and stewards of the mysteries of God."

Paul is always referring to mysteries that were revealed to him. And what are mysteries? Secrets. And Who kept them secret until revealed to this man? God did. When God called Paul out of the religion of Judaism, and saved him on the road to Damascus, He sent him to Mt. Sinai and poured out on him for three years all the revelations of the mysteries. There are all kinds of mysteries that Paul speaks of in his writings, and since they were revealed to him, he then became the steward (administrator) of those mysteries. Some of the mysteries may have been prophesied to some small degree in the Old Testament, but no one comprehended them until they were revealed to Paul. See Chapter "MYSTERIES" to see some of the other things God revealed to Paul and no other man before. Better yet, read all of Paul's thirteen epistles, Romans to Philemon; practically all of which is mystery. Our salvation is included. Jesus and the twelve could not preach Jesus' death, burial, and resurrection for salvation, because it hadn't happened yet.

Jesus, the promised Messiah came; the Nation of Israel was in the promised land; they had the temple, but yet, what did they do with the Messiah. They crucified Him; and the Jews continued to reject Him in those early chapters of "ACTS". A few Jews thought they would soon go through the seven-year tribulation and then Jesus would return as their Messiah and set up His Kingdom, His 1000-year reign on earth (Millennium). Instead, because of their unbelief as a Nation, God set Israel aside in His time line, and inserted the present 2000-year dispensation of

Grace, to call out a people for His Name. All the things that the Law demanded, Jesus provided on the Cross.

Galatians 3:21b *"...if there had been a law given which could have given life, verily righteousness should have been by the law."*

The law could not save.

This dispensation of Grace was given to Paul for him to dispense to the Gentiles mainly, and to the Jews, and to all the world. Paul calls it "his Gospel".

Romans 16:25 *"Now to him that is of power to establish you* (believers) *according to* (the Gospel? No; what?) *my gospel and the preaching of Jesus Christ, according to the revelation* (or revealing) *of the mystery* (the secret that's been kept in the mind of God), *which was kept secret since the world began."*

Acts 20:24 *"But none of these things move me* (Paul), *neither count I my life dear unto myself, so that I might finish my course with joy, and the ministry, which I have received of the Lord Jesus, to testify the gospel of the Grace of God."*

Paul's whole ministry was to proclaim the Gospel of the Grace of God. So all we've got to do to be saved is believe Paul's Gospel.

Very few people have any idea of the Grace of God. God loved the human race. He took on human flesh, walked among men for three years on the dusty roads of Israel, and then ended up going to the Cross to suffer the most horrible death ever invented, all because of His love for mankind. And through that death on the Cross, He was able to pay the price of redemption for the whole human race; not just a few chosen ones, but for the whole race. Now listen; that's GRACE!

***Ephesians 2:5** "Even when we were dead in sins,* (God) *hath quickened* (made alive) *us together with Christ, (by grace ye are saved;)"*

***Ephesians 2:8,9** "For by grace are ye saved through faith, and that not of yourselves: it is the gift of God: Not of works, lest any man should boast."*

***Romans 6:14** "For sin shall not have dominion over you: for ye are not under the law, but under grace."*

***Romans 5:20,21** "Moreover the law entered, that the offence might abound. But where sin abounded, grace did much more abound; That as sin hath reigned unto death, even so might grace reign through righteousness unto eternal life by Jesus Christ our Lord."*

When the law was given, sin became more prevalent. Then grace came and was much more prevalent. As sin led to death, grace now leads us to salvation, the righteousness of God, and to eternal life through Jesus Christ, our Saviour and Lord.

***Galatians 5:4** "Christ is become of no effect unto you, whosoever of you are justified by the law, ye are fallen from grace."*

You cannot be saved by the grace of God and then live by the law. Law and grace don't mix.

When something negative happens in our lives, someone may make statements like the following to us:

> Well, your sins are finding you out!
>
> I knew it – the rooster has come home to roost!
>
> You're reaping what you've sown!

Today, we do not reap what we have sown. Under the Gospel of Grace, we sow nothing, but through Jesus, we reap every blessing. That's GRACE!

The law condemns the sinner – grace redeems the sinner.

The law curses – grace blesses.

The law reveals sin – grace atones for sin.

The law was done away in Christ – grace abides forever.

The dispensation of Law was given through Moses to Israel.

The dispensation of Grace was given through the apostle Paul to the Gentiles.

Chapter 5

PETER'S GOSPEL VERSUS PAUL'S GOSPEL

Acts 9:15a *"But the Lord said unto him* (Ananias) *Go thy way;* (to Paul) *for he is a chosen vessel unto me, to bear my name before the Gentiles,…"*

The Lord had saved Paul on the road to Damascus and told him to preach the Gospel to the Gentiles (us).

Galatians 1:11 *"But I certify you, brethren, that the gospel which was preached of me is not after man."*

Galatians 1:12 *"For I neither received it of man, neither was I taught it, But by the revelation of Jesus Christ."*

Paul didn't go to Jerusalem to be taught by the twelve disciples, but was called to Mt. Sinai to receive of the Lord a new Gospel, the Gospel of the Grace of God.

Acts 16:30 "*And brought them* (Paul and Silas) *out, and said, Sirs, what must I do to be saved?*"

Acts 16:31 "*And they* (Paul and Silas) *said, 'Believe on the Lord Jesus Christ, and thou shalt be saved, and thy house.'*"

Here, Paul and Silas were in prison, and the pagan Gentile jailer asked how to be saved. Paul's message was to believe that Jesus died on the Cross, was buried and rose from the dead. You can search Paul's epistles from "Romans" to "Hebrews" and you won't find one place where Paul teaches repentance and baptism for salvation.

Acts 3:24,25 "*Yea, and all the prophets from Samuel and those that follow, as many as have spoken, have like-wise foretold of these days.*"

What days? Everything that has just taken place. According to Peter, the Crucifixion, Resurrection, Ascension, and coming of the Holy Spirit were prophesied.

Now *verse 25:* "*Ye are the children of the prophets, and of the covenant* (only the Nation of Israel. All prophecy is directed to the Nation of Israel; they are the ones who will be at the core of these prophetic events. Even the horrible events in "Revelation" will be directed primarily at the Jew. But, the whole world will also reap the fallout from these events) *which God made with our fathers, saying unto Abraham, and in thy seed* (through the Nation of Israel) *shall all the kindreds of the earth be blessed.*"

So Peter is on Covenant ground. He's still on the basis that everything that has been prophesied since Abraham will be, that is: the Nation of Israel was to receive the Redeemer, the Messiah, the King and the Kingdom, and it would be through Israel that God would gather the Gentiles. God was going to use the Nation of Israel on Covenant grounds to bring the Gentiles to salvation.

Acts 2:36 "Therefore let all the house of Israel (Peter is talking to Jew only) *know assuredly, that God hath made that same Jesus, whom ye have crucified, both Lord and Christ."*

Here, Peter is accusing the Nation of Israel of killing their Messiah.

Galatians 1:3,4a "Grace be to you and peace from God the Father, and from our Lord Jesus Christ, Who gave himself for our sins...."

Jesus' death and shedding of His blood for our sins is Paul's theme all through his writings. Now back to Acts, verse 37:

Acts 2:37 "Now when they heard this (heard what? That they were guilty; of crucifying their Messiah. Peter is talking to thousands of Jews who have come to celebrate the Feast of Pentecost) *they were pricked in their hearts* (convicted)*, and said unto Peter and to the rest of the apostles, Men and brethren what shall we do?"*

Notice the "we do". The question is coming from the Nation of Israel. Covenants were to the Nation of Israel. Whereas, the jailer asked Paul, "What shall I do?" God dealt with the Jews as a Nation before, but now deals with individuals. Salvation is a personal experience between you and God.

Acts 2:38 "Then Peter said unto them 'Repent, and be baptized, every one of you in the name of Jesus Christ for the remission of sins, and ye shall receive the gift of the Holy Ghost.'"

Not a word here about the death, burial and resurrection, which on the other hand is the crux of Paul's gospel. Every one of them would have to be converted and accept Christ as their Messiah for God to pick up where He had left off. He would have sent back the King and set up His Kingdom. The Jews rejected Jesus then, and even to this day, do not accept Jesus Christ as their Messiah. So God called Paul to go to the Gentiles to call out a people for His name. That's where we are today; have been for the past 2000 years, but this Age of Grace is about to come to a close, so get saved and look up – your redemption draweth nigh.

To the Jew, Salvation was "repent and be baptized".
To the Gentile, Salvation is "believe the Gospel".

Peter's gospel, called the gospel of the kingdom or the gospel of circumcision, was preached to the Nation of Israel under the Law of Moses.

Paul's gospel, called the gospel of grace or the gospel of uncircumcision, was, and is being, preached to the Gentiles under the grace of God.

Paul, several times, went to Jerusalem to share with Peter some of the new revelations he had received from God, but Peter never did comprehend them all.

Galatians 2:7 *"But contrariwise, when they* (the leadership of the Jerusalem Jewish assembly) *saw that the gospel of the uncircumcision* (non-Jewish world; us) *was committed unto me* (Paul) *as the gospel of the circumcision (Jewish world) was to Peter:"*

Then in *verse 9* *"James, Cephas* (Peter) *and John gave to me* (Paul) *and Barnabas the right hands of fellowship; that we should go unto the heathen* (us) *and they unto the circumcision."*

It is obvious that Peter's gospel and Paul's gospel are so different that there is no way you can mix them. If you do, you will never understand either.

Most preaching and Sunday School material today comes from the four Gospels which is okay to a degree, but that all took place before the work of the Cross. Paul preached salvation based on what Jesus did on the Cross. Paul told the Romans in Romans 16:25 that they were established according to "my gospel" and that which he preached concerning Jesus Christ, according to the revelation of the mystery, which was kept secret since the world began. Peter couldn't preach the Gospel of Grace because it wasn't revealed to Paul until several years later.

Paul's gospel is the way, the only way, of salvation for us in this present age of Grace. It is open for anyone who will believe, even the Jew.

Chapter 6

SALVATION NOT BY

The apostle Paul tells the saints of Ephesus that after they heard the word of truth, the gospel that he preached; and believed it, then they were saved; by grace, through faith and not of themselves: it is a free gift of God, not of works, lest any man should boast.

Today, instead of obtaining God's righteousness by putting our faith in what Jesus Christ did on the Cross, we mistakenly try to earn salvation and self-righteousness by our own works, which may include:

Living a good life.

Doing what seems right.

Doing the best we can.

Doing good works.

Praying through (to what?).

Forgiving others.

Repentance.

Telling God we're sorry for our sins.

Begging God to forgive us our sins.

Asking God to be merciful to me, a sinner.

Asking the Father to send the Holy Spirit into our hearts to reveal sins to us.

Continually asking God to forgive our sins (like asking Jesus to shed some more blood).

Giving to churches and charities.

Giving 10% of our income.

Ritual.

Following man's traditions.

Law keeping (Ten Commandments).

Temple worship.

Faith in Jesus' life on earth.

Faith in Jesus' three years of exemplar miracle working.

Baptism in water.

Church membership and attendance.

Speaking in tongues.

Any gospel, other than Paul's.

Some of these things are okay, but will come after salvation, and not be used to bring a person to righteousness.

As far as salvation is concerned, we don't have to ask God the Father for anything; Jesus has done it all on the Cross. When He said "It is finished", that's exactly what He meant. All we have to do is BELIEVE.

Chapter 7

THINK THEY'RE SAVED

There are countless millions who are so hung up on tradition, and they base their very eternal destination on some of these traditions. Traditions are some things that have been passed down from generation to generation, and many never bother to check the Scripture to see if these traditions are really true for the Body of Christ believer. How can they be so gullible when thirteen books of the New Testament, written by the Apostle Paul for the Body of Christ, give us "can't miss instructions" for eternal life.

I Corinthians 2:14 *"But the natural man* (the unbeliever; I don't care if he's in church every Sunday. If he's still unsaved and in the natural, he) *receiveth not the things of the Spirit of God;* (it's impossible for him. Why?) *for they are foolishness* (not understandable) *unto him: neither can he know them, because they are spiritually discerned."*

I Corinthians 1:18 *"For the preaching of the cross is to them that perish foolishness, but unto us which are saved, it is the power of God."*

41

The Cross is being left out of most of what is being taught today. No one can be saved by simply believing in Jesus. James says the devils also believe in one God and they tremble. Believing has to be in the work of the Cross. The Gospel; that Christ died, was buried, and rose again.

Today, too much of Christianity is using clichés. You have heard the expression, "Well, I've accepted the Lord Jesus as my personal Saviour." There is nothing wrong with that, but what is it? It's a coined phrase. It's not in the Bible! You show me one verse where it says that if you will take Jesus as your Lord and personal Saviour, that you will be saved. Now, if you take the Lord Jesus Christ as your personal Saviour, based on the fact that He, the very Son of God, became flesh, went to the Cross, shed His blood, died, was buried, and rose from the dead, and put that whole truth into your cliché, then I have no problem with that.

Another cliché is: "Well, if you'll just take Jesus into your heart." The only reason you can have Jesus in your heart, is because you believe He died for you on that Cross.

We might say, Well, my grandma was "a certain denomination" or "we go to a certain church." Salvation is a personal, individual relationship with God. Every man stands on his own. God does not have grand-children; only children.

Another cliché we like to use is, "Well, if you just believe in Jesus."

II Corinthians 5:16 *"Wherefore henceforth know we no man after the flesh: yea, though we have known Christ after the flesh, yet now henceforth know we Him no more."*

Paul is telling us that even though we are aware of the three-year earthly ministry of Christ to Israel, we should not be concerned with it; but that which we should be concerned with is the part of Christ's life where He went to the Cross to provide for our salvation.

People are being led into a false security by simply taking short cuts, or clichés, without knowing the full truth of the matter. So we are saved by the power of God, from the preaching of the Cross.

Paul feared, lest by any means, as the serpent beguiled Eve through his subtilty, that the minds of the Corinthians might be corrupted from the simplicity that is in Christ. For if someone came to them preaching a Jesus other than the One Paul preached, or if they received another spirit other than the one indwelling them, or another gospel which they had not received, they might fall for it. Paul called these preachers false apostles, deceitful workers, transforming themselves into the apostles of Christ.

II Corinthians 11:14,15 *"And no marvel; for Satan himself is transformed into an angel of light. Therefore it is no great thing if his ministers also be transformed as the ministers of righteousness; whose end shall be according to their works."*

If you didn't get saved by Paul's Gospel of Salvation, you are not saved.

Preachers out there; are you teaching true doctrine, Jesus and Him Crucified, or are you instruments in the hands of Satan, spewing false doctrine throughout the world and leading people to Hell?

Galatians 3:10 "For as many as are of the works of the law are under the curse: for it is written, cursed is every one that continueth not in all things which are written in the book of the law to do them."

Matthew 7:22,23 Many will say, Lord, Lord, have we not cast out devils, prophesied, and done wonderful works in thy name? Jesus will say "Depart from me, I never knew you, ye that work iniquity."

Proverbs 14:12 "There is a way which seemeth right unto a man, but the end thereof are the ways of death."

I Corinthians 10:12 "Wherefore let him that thinketh he standeth take heed lest he fall."

Most of the above scriptures pertain to you who think you're saved. Make your salvation sure by believing on the one true Gospel, JESUS AND HIM CRUCIFIED.

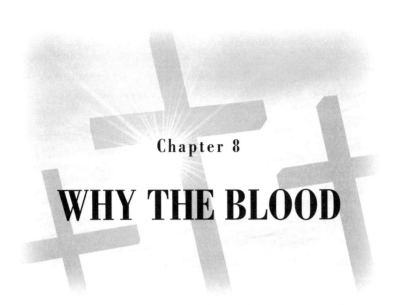

Chapter 8

WHY THE BLOOD

Colossians 1:14 "In whom (the Son) *we have redemption through his blood, even the forgiveness of sin:"*

Hebrews 9:22 "And almost all things are by the law (back in the sacrificial economy) *purged with blood; and without shedding of blood is no remission."*

Without the shedding of blood there has never been any forgiveness of sin. Back in the Garden of Eden when Adam and Eve first sinned, God killed animals, a blood sacrifice, to clothe and restore them.

Satan counterfeits everything good in God's economy. Even in the uncivilized areas of the world; in the Satanic rituals; animals, birds, and sometimes children were and are being killed for a blood sacrifice. This is Satan's counterfeit.

God perfected the system of blood sacrifice with the Law and the Temple worship. Jesus was our supreme Sacrifice when He shed

His blood and died on the Cross. He shed His blood for the forgiveness of our sins. There is no more need for sacrifice since Jesus' death.

The blood, to be effective, had to be applied. Back when the children of Israel were being delivered from Egypt, they had to apply the lambs' sacrificial blood to the sides and lintels of the doorways of their abodes in order for the death angel to pass over them. In the Old Testament, the high priest went into the Holy of Holies, once a year, to apply sacrificial animal blood to the mercy seat of the Ark of the Covenant, for the covering of the sins of the people.

After His death, Jesus became our High Priest forever, after the order of Melchisedec.

Hebrews 9:12 *"Neither by the blood of goats and calves, but by his own blood he entered in once into the holy place, having obtained eternal redemption for us."*

Jesus presented His own blood in the very Throne Room of Heaven as our High Priest, that we may have eternal redemption.

If the sprinkling of the blood on the mercy seat in the Old Testament covered the sins of the people for a year, how much more can the blood of Christ cover our sins for all eternity? The Bible says Jesus took away our sins, which sins will never be remembered again.

Chapter 9

SALVATION IN "OLD TESTAMENT" TIMES

Abraham believed God, and it was imputed unto him for righteousness.

Galatians 3:7 ***"Knowing ye therefore that they which are of faith,*** (in other words, those of us who have entered into a salvation experience by faith only) ***the same are the children*** (or the sons) ***of Abraham."***

Today we are saved by faith.

Genesis 13:16a ***"And I will make thy seed*** (the offspring) ***as the dust of the earth:..."***

Dust is earthly and Abraham's earthly (fleshly) progeny came by the physical offspring (Jews – the nation of Israel) by Abraham's sons, Isaac and Jacob.

Genesis 15:5 *"And he* (God) ***brought him*** (Abraham) ***forth abroad, and said, Look now toward heaven, and*** (count or) ***tell the stars, if thou be able to number them, and he said unto him, So shall thy seed be. "***

This is the heavenly (spiritual) connection to Abraham, which are those who have entered in like he did by faith, and faith alone. This is us today.

So, on the time line we have Abraham 2000 years after Adam, and 2000 years before Christ. From Abraham to the Cross we have the history of Abraham's earthly progeny, the Jews (Israel), God's chosen people through which the Saviour of the world would come. Up until the Cross, the Gentiles (people other than Jews) have hardly been dealt with by God, or mentioned, except as "dogs" by the Jews.

How did people from Adam to Abraham come into a right relationship with God; faith plus nothing? No way; but rather it was faith plus sacrifice. They couldn't approach God without the sacrifice. Coming up to the Cross, even in Christ's three-year earthly ministry, did Jesus ever teach the concept of a salvation by faith and faith alone? No! What were they to do? They were still to be adherent to the Law of Moses; they also had the added responsibility of repentance and water baptism, plus their faith in Who Jesus was. But faith alone wouldn't cut it. Even in the early chapters of the book of "Acts", early years after Christ died on the Cross, it wasn't just faith and faith alone. They had to repent and be baptized for the remission of sins and had to believe that Jesus (the One they crucified) was the Son of God and their Messiah.

Back, when they were still in Egypt, God called the Nation of Israel out as His chosen people, His son, His favored nation; out of whom would come the Saviour of the world. He gave them the Covenant promises.

From the time of their delivery from Egypt up to the time of the Cross and even after, the people of Israel were faithless; always complaining, and rejecting the things of God.

God dealt with Israel in the Old Testament years through the prophets. What did they do to the prophets? They refused to hear them and killed them. Next, God sent His Son, the Christ, and Jesus the Christ presented Himself to the Nation of Israel as coming to fulfill the promises made to the fathers. And what did they do to the Son? They rejected Him as their Messiah and had Him Crucified (the Cross). In the first part of the book of Acts, the higher-ups in the synagogue stoned Stephen to death. Stephen was a type of the Holy Spirit. So the Nation of Israel essentially had rejected the Godhead; the Father, the Son, and the Holy Spirit.

Matthew 21:43 "Therefore, say I (God) *unto you* (Israel) *'The kingdom of God shall be taken from you, and given to a nation* (Gentiles) *bringing forth the fruits thereof.'"*

ACTS: The four Gospel writers – Matthew, Mark, Luke and John – have just finished recording the earthly life of Jesus, ending with His resurrection and promise to send the Holy Spirit. In His 33 years on earth, Jesus had been born under the Old Covenant, lived His life under it, and in His death fulfilled it.

Acts 1:3 For forty days after His death on the Cross, Jesus showed Himself alive to His disciples by many infallible proofs, and spoke to them of the things pertaining to the Kingdom of God.

Peter preached the gospel of the kingdom; repent and be baptized. If the Nation of Israel would have believed Whom He was, Jesus would have returned and set up His Kingdom. But they continued to reject Him, and as a result, Israel has, for the last 2000 years, been going through suffering, turmoil, in a state of spiritual blindness (Romans 11:25).

Just after the death of Stephen, about seven years after Pentecost, God set Israel aside and Jesus saved Saul of Tarsus (Paul) and commissioned him to preach the Gospel of Christ to Gentiles, to call out a people for His name. Of course, this gospel is for the Jew as well. The apostle Paul referred to this gospel as "My Gospel", because Jesus had personally given this Gospel to him and none other. This Gospel is the one, and only one, by which we are saved today. It is Christ and Him Crucified; the Cross and what Jesus accomplished for us on that Cross. This 2000 year period, the Age of Grace, is about over. The end will be evidenced by the Rapture of the Church, at which time God's time line will revert back to Israel and the Gospel of the Kingdom.

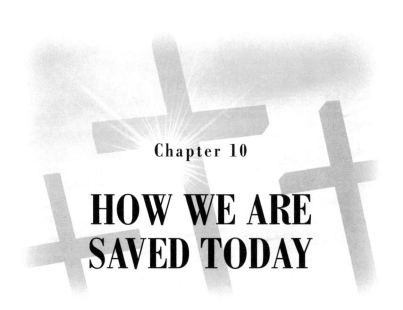

Chapter 10

HOW WE ARE SAVED TODAY

Romans 3:23 "For all have sinned and come short of the glory of God;"

We inherited the sinful nature from Adam.

Romans 6:23a "For the wages of sin is death;..."

This death is eternal separation from God, and we will spend it in the Lake of Fire with Satan.

Romans 6:23b "...but the gift of God is eternal life through Jesus Christ our Lord."

Before the beginning of time, God, because of His love for mankind, had a plan whereby sinful man could be brought back into fellowship with Him. This fellowship had been broken because of Adam's sin. God, being Holy, could not look upon sin.

This plan was that God would send His Son, Jesus Christ, as a man, to shed His blood for the taking away of our sins, to die on the Cross in our place for the penalty of sin, be buried, and be raised the third day.

Since Adam, God has dealt with mankind in various ways. Salvation has been by conscience, sacrifice, law, and grace.

Righteousness (right standing with God) was imputed to Abraham because he believed God. He had faith that what God told him, God was able to perform. This is the same way we obtain salvation today – by faith, not in what Jesus could perform, but in what Jesus did do for us on the Cross.

From Moses to John, the Baptist, salvation was by the Mosaic Law; keeping the Law (which was impossible), temple worship, and the sacrificing of animals.

When John the Baptist came on the scene as the forerunner of Jesus, he preached "repent and be baptized for the remission of sins." This message, along with the requirement that the Jews would recognize Jesus as their Messiah (the Son of God) was called "The Gospel of the Kingdom." If the Nation of Israel had accepted Jesus as such, the Tribulation period of seven years would have taken place and then Jesus would have set up the 1000-year kingdom and the Jews would have presented their King to the Gentile world. But they rejected Jesus and had Him Crucified.

About eight years after the Cross, God set the Nation of Israel aside, and turned to the Gentiles (us), through the apostle Paul, to call out a people for His name. This period of time, called the

Age of Grace, has been on going for approximately 2000 years and could come to an end any day. Salvation is by believing on Jesus and what He did for us on the Cross. This salvation is a free gift, obtained only by believing; not of works, lest any man should boast. This is how we are saved today; by the Gospel of Grace.

The Nation of Israel not only rejected Jesus and had Him crucified, but they continued to follow the Mosaic law, attempting to establish their own righteousness by their own works.

This is where the worldly church is today; living just like the Nation of Israel, putting emphasis on keeping the law, on their own works instead of the finished work of the Cross, and seeking salvation by the Gospel of the Kingdom. The majority of sermons preached today are taken from the four gospel accounts and the first part of "Acts", and the people are mislead and defeated. The gospel accounts of Matthew, Mark, Luke, and John and parts of Acts can be more aptly considered as Old Testament books in that they are mostly about Israel's prophecy program, "that which was spoken". They are Jewish books, concerning Israel and Judaism. They are not for us today. We see law-keeping honored and taught throughout these books. Also, the events of Pentecost are not for us today. They, too, were the subject of prophecy; they had been spoken and foretold by God.

Romans 15:8 *"...Jesus Christ was a minister of the circumcision* (Jews) *for the truth of God, to confirm the promises made unto the fathers:"*

Today, our Lord is no longer a minister to the circumcision as He was in the gospel accounts, but is the Head of the Church, the Body of Christ.

Paul's Gospel is the Gospel, (not a gospel, but) the only Gospel by which we are saved today. Not by anything taught or preached in the Old Testament or during the time of Christ's earthly ministry. Not by anything taught by the twelve or even that taught by Jesus. Paul says, though we have known Christ after the flesh, henceforth know we Him no more. In other words, even though we are aware of everything He came for and accomplished in Jerusalem; what we are to be concerned with now is what He accomplished for us on the Cross. That is, receive Him (know Him) as Saviour and Lord.

Now that we have been given a synopsis of events in the past leading up to the Gospel of Grace, let us backtrack to our position as a sinner and proceed from there.

Jesus is Light. Jesus said that men love darkness rather than light. Adam and Eve, when they sinned, hid from God. No sinner ever goes looking for God – God always looks for the sinner. No man comes to God on his own prerogative; the Father must draw him (I John 6:44). You are reading this chapter (salvation) in this book. It is not by accident – the Holy Spirit has been wooing you; and leading you to this very moment. Don't let it be for naught.

The law has been mentioned several times as being the downfall of, and failure of a person attempting to live a Christian life. All through Paul's epistles, he warns us against mixing law and grace. When you mix law and grace, you become confused, and the benefits of both are nullified.

We are saved by the Grace of God; not by law.

Galatians 2:21 *"I do not frustrate the grace of God: for if righteousness come by the law, then Christ is dead in vain."*

Galatians 5:1 *"Stand fast therefore, in the liberty wherewith Christ hath made us free, and be not entangled again with the yoke of bondage* (law).*"*

Galatians 3:11 *"But that no man is justified by the law in the sight of God, it is evident: for, the just shall live by faith."*

Galatians 3:10a *"For as many as are of the works of the law are under the curse:..."*

Galatians 3:13a *"Christ hath redeemed us from the curse of the law, being made a curse for us:..."*

Galatians 5:4 *"Christ is become of no effect unto you, whosoever of you are justified by the law; ye are fallen from grace."*

Romans 4:5 *"But to him that worketh not, but believeth on him* (Jesus) *that justifieth the ungodly, his faith is counted for righteousness."*

Romans 4:24 *"But for us also, to whom it* (righteousness) *shall be imputed, if we believe on him that raised up Jesus our Lord from the dead;"*

Romans 5:19 *"For as by one man's* (Adam's) *disobedience, many were made sinners, so by the obedience* (Crucifixion) *of one* (Jesus) *shall many be made righteous."*

Romans 5:21 "That as sin hath reigned unto death, even so might grace reign through righteousness unto eternal life by Jesus Christ our Lord."

Romans 9:30 "What shall we say then? That the Gentiles (us) *which followed not after righteousness, have attained to righteousness, even the righteousness which is of faith* (in the Cross).*"*

Romans 9:31 "But Israel, which followed after the law of righteousness, hath not attained to the law of righteousness."

Romans 9:32 "Wherefore? Because they sought it not by faith, but as it were by the works of the law (we are doing the same thing today).* For they stumbled at the stumbling-stone* (the Cross);*"*

Now, let me say a word or two to the Jew; to the Nation of Israel. In the Book of Romans, the apostle Paul states that his heart's desire and his prayer is that Israel be saved. Even though Israel has a zeal of God, they are ignorant of God's righteousness and are going about to establish their own righteousness by their law-keeping and good works. Righteousness is a gift because of what Jesus has accomplished on the Cross for you. All your sins – past, present, and future – have been washed clean by His precious blood. You are completely forgiven, and from the moment you receive Jesus into your life, you will never be held liable for your sins, ever again. You have been made righteous as Jesus, not through your behavior, but by your faith in Him and His finished work on the Cross. God says in Romans, that He has reserved 7000 men to be saved according to the election of grace; not by works, but by grace. The rest of Israel will be blinded, in part, until the fulness of the Gentiles be come in (the Rapture).

Many church goers, like the Jews in the preceding paragraph, are mislead and defeated today because they also, are trying to earn their own righteousness by their law-keeping and good works.

II Corinthians 5:21 *"For he* (God) *hath made him* (Jesus) *to be sin for us, who* (Jesus) *knew no sin; that we might be made the righteousness of God in him* (Jesus).*"*

We, today, are automatically made righteous, the moment we believe on Jesus and the Cross. Christ takes our sins and gives His righteousness to us who believe. Before we are saved, our righteousness is as filthy rags. The Cross of Jesus changes everything when we are saved. Jesus receives all our bad, our sins and unrighteousness, and we take all His "good", His right-eousness. That's the Gospel of Jesus Christ. It is based entirely on His Grace.

As we have just shown, the moment we are saved, we are made the righteousness of God in Christ. When we are saved, our sins (past, present, and future) are forgiven us. Our sin debt has been paid by the shedding of Jesus' blood at Calvary (Colossians 1:14). We become children of God (Romans 8:16). We have been given eternal life (Romans 6:23b). Think of it; eternal life, forever and forever with our Saviour, Jesus Christ.

At salvation, the love of God is shed abroad in our hearts by the Holy Ghost, which is given unto us (Romans 5:5). Ephesians 1:13 tells us that the moment we believe for salvation, we are sealed with the Holy Spirit of God; which makes us God's for all eternity.

This seal is God's guarantee that our salvation is eternal (Ephesians 4:30).

Upon salvation, the Holy Spirit baptizes us into the Body of Christ, and being baptized into Jesus Christ, we are baptized into His death (Romans 6:3). Our old man is crucified (put to death) with Christ, that the body of sin might be destroyed, that henceforth we should not serve sin (Romans 6:6). For he that is dead is freed from sin (Romans 6:7). Sin shall not have dominion over you; for you are not under the law, but under grace (Romans 6:14). Where sin abounded, grace did much more abound (Romans 5:20). Being made free from sin, we become the servants of righteousness to God, and the end everlasting life (Romans 6:18,22). We, as believers, also are become dead to the law by the body of Christ (Romans 7:4a). There is therefore no condemnation to them which are in Christ Jesus (Romans 8:1).

From the above, you might ask, "Well, if we are considered forever righteous and our sins, even our future sins, will never, ever be held against us, and there is no condemnation to us who are in Christ Jesus, won't that cause us to want to sin more, knowing we can get away with it?" No way! Sin loses its appeal every time we think of Jesus Christ, Who loved us so much that He was beaten, shed His blood, and died that we might be forgiven completely and have everlasting life. We realize that we have been given this great gift of righteousness which we did nothing to deserve, earn, or merit. Now what happens? We will fall in love with Jesus all over again and it will make us better persons at whatever we do. Instead of willfully committing sin, we will want to glorify our Lord Jesus Christ by living a life that is pleasing to Him and that is victorious over sin.

I Corinthians 15:34a *"Awake to righteousness, and sin not;..."*

Further, if someone has really known and experienced grace and the gift of "no condemnation", he will NOT want to live in sin. Sin will be the last thing on his mind. Anyone who is living in sin is not under grace and has not experienced the gift of no condemnation. Grace always results in victory over sin.

Galatians 14:9 Paul says to the Galatians, Now that you have known God, how can you return to the weak and beggarly elements (the things you were saved out of) where unto you desire again to be in bondage (keeping of the law)?

He is a fool who would desire health so that he might with it be sick also.

He is a fool who would abide still in the fire, that he might be delivered from burning.

So also, he is a fool, who desiring to be dead unto sin, thinks he may yet live in it.

Peter says that if we turn away from the way of righteousness after we have known it, we are like the dog who returns to his own vomit, and the sow that was washed, to her wallowing in the mire.

Once we have been redeemed out of Satan's slave market and have come into the Grace of God, and comprehend all that Christ has done for us on the Cross, how can we help but want to serve Him.

When we say that we are saved by the works Jesus did on the Cross, it is important to include and recognize the "resurrection of the dead" as part of that Cross. If there is no resurrection of the dead, then Christ is not risen. And, if Christ is not risen, Paul says, then our preaching is vain, and our faith is also vain; we are still in our sins. They which are fallen asleep (died physically) in Christ are perished. If in this life only, we have hope in Christ, we are of all men most miserable.

Romans 1:4 *"Jesus was declared to be the Son of God, with power, according to the Spirit of holiness, by the resurrection from the dead:"*

But NOW, Christ is risen from the dead, and become the first fruits of them that slept. The dead in Christ and we which are alive will be caught up to meet Christ in the air when He comes for us in the Rapture, and we will be with Him forever. For in Adam all die; even so, in Christ, all shall be made alive.

As I said before, Paul's gospel, today, is the gospel, the only gospel, by which we are saved. Paul told the Galatians that the gospel which he preached was not received from man, but was revealed to him by Jesus Christ, the risen LORD of Glory (Galatians 1:11,12).

Paul was having trouble with Judaizers coming to the churches he had established and teaching false doctrine to his converts. He besought them to mark the ones who were causing divisions and offences contrary to the doctrines they had learned from him; and to avoid them. Just as the Judaizers were pushing circumcision, keeping of the law, water baptism, and so forth, back then; Satan is perverting the Gospel today.

Galatians 1:8 "But though we, or an angel from heaven, preach any other gospel unto you than that ye have received, let him be accursed."

Galatians 1:9 "As we said before, so say I now again, if any man preach any other gospel unto you than that ye have received, let him be accursed."

These two verses tell me that, if any one preaches salvation by any other gospel than Paul's, he might find himself in the hottest corner of the Lake of Fire.

Paul calls these false teachers false apostles, deceitful workers; transforming themselves unto the apostles of Christ. And no wonder, for Satan himself is transformed into an angel of light. Therefore it is no great thing if his (Satan's) ministers also be transformed as the ministers of righteousness; whose end shall be according to their works (II Corinthians 11:13-15). Remember, back in Genesis, Satan, in the form of a serpent, beguiled Eve through his subtlety, by telling her when she ate of the forbidden tree, she would be as gods. Satan's ministers are hard at work today corrupting the minds of the people from the simplicity that is in Christ. We need to be careful, what we listen to, and what we read. Any time we are hearing the Word of God, we need to compare, and if it doesn't agree with that which the apostle Paul teaches, avoid it.

Romans 1:16 "For I am not ashamed of the gospel of Christ: for it is the power of God unto salvation to every-one that believeth; to the Jew first, and also to the Greek."

Paul didn't say, "To everyone who repents and is baptized" or "to everyone who does according to man's traditions", but he said "to everyone that believeth!" He stated very plainly that if we believe this Gospel with all our hearts – that Christ died, was buried and rose from the dead – then that Gospel becomes the very power of God Himself. The very power that created the universe is released to us, on us, and in us so that we, by that power of God, become the children of God. It is beyond human understanding, so we must take it by faith. The Bible says that is what the Gospel is, and when we believe it, God counts it as righteousness for us. But it is imperative that we be very careful what we believe.

I Timothy 2:4 It is God's will that all men be saved, and come unto the knowledge of the truth.

II Corinthians 6:2b *"...Now is the day of salvation."*

Before salvation, we walked according to the course of this world; according to Satan, the spirit that worketh in the children of disobedience. Among whom we all had our conversation (way of life) in times past in the lusts of the flesh, fulfilling the desires of the flesh and of the mind; and were, by nature the children of wrath (Ephesians 2:2,3).

Some of us in times past received salvation through the teachings of pastors who preached everything except Paul's gospel. The way of salvation was similar to the gospel of the kingdom which Jesus and the twelve preached. Salvation scriptures included John 3:16, Acts 2:21, Mark 16:16 and others, that if you endured to the end, you would be saved. These scriptures are all Jewish and they don't mention the death of Jesus Christ and the shedding of His blood. Without the shedding of blood, there is no remission of sin.

Today, we live in the dispensation of the Grace of God. The Gospel of the Grace of God, given to the apostle Paul to us, is the only gospel by which we are saved. The dispensation of the Grace of God and the Gospel of the Grace of God cannot be found in the scriptures before Christ revealed them to Paul, at least eight years after Pentecost.

The accomplishments of Christ's finished work on the Cross are not fully known or made manifest until revealed to and preached by Paul.

Paul tells us why God kept the age of grace a secret, in I Corinthians 2:7,8, "for if the princes of this world had known it, they would not have crucified the Lord of Glory." If Satan had known, he would not have crucified our Lord and we would still be in our sins, our faith would be in vain, and there would be no hope for any of us.

God, Who is rich in mercy, for His great love wherewith He loved us, even when we were dead in sins, hath quickened (made alive) us together with Christ, (by grace ye are saved); and has raised us up together, and made us sit together in heavenly places in Christ Jesus. For by grace are ye saved through faith, not of yourselves (anything you can do to merit it); it is the gift of God. Not of works, lest any man should boast. At salvation we are now made nigh unto God, not by covenants which were made to the Jews, but by the precious blood of Jesus Christ (Ephesians 2:4-13).

Philippians 2:7-11 Jesus took upon Himself the form of a servant, in the likeness of man, and as a man He became obedient unto death, even the death of the Cross. Wherefore, God highly exalted Him and gave Him a name, which is above every name; that at that name of Jesus every knee will bow and every tongue will confess that Jesus Christ is Lord, to the glory of God the Father.

Are you going to confess Him today and live eternally with Him or are you going to reject Him, stand before Him later at the Great White Throne Judgment (confess Him then, but it will be too late), and be sentenced to an eternal existence in the Lake of Fire?

Actually, providing salvation for us today was expensive. It cost God the death of His Son and our Saviour Jesus Christ. But, the receiving of that salvation is quite simple. All the other Chapters of this book, as well as everything in this Chapter have been included for our understanding. I feel all is related, although some remotely to salvation and will help us make a positive decision for Christ, and when we do, know somewhat that which has happened to us and in us, and enable us to grasp things and to grow in grace more rapidly.

Romans 5:8 But God commendeth His love toward us in that, while we were yet sinners, Christ died for us."

God sent His Son to be the propitiation, not only for our sins, but for the sins of the world. Propitiation sounds like a big word, but it simply means that Jesus' death, and the shedding of His blood satisfied God's just demands of holiness for the punishment of sin. In other words, by His death on the Cross, Jesus became sin for us, that we might be made the righteousness of God in Him (II Corinthians 5:21).

***Ephesians 2:8,9** "For by grace are ye saved through faith, and that not of yourselves: it is the gift of God: Not of works, lest any man should boast."*

***Romans 1:4** "Jesus Christ was declared to be the Son of God with power, according to the spirit of holiness, by the resurrection from the dead."*

Jesus Christ not only died for our sins, but was raised for our justification (Romans 4:25).

***I Corinthians 15:20** "But now is Christ risen from the dead, and become the firstfruits of them that slept."*

And at the time of the Rapture, those who have died in Christ and we which are alive in Christ will put on incorruption and immortality, and be resurrected to meet Jesus in the air and forever be with Him.

***I Corinthians 15:3b,4** "Christ died for our sins according to the scriptures; And that he was buried, and that he rose again the third day according to the scriptures:"*

This is God's Gospel for salvation. All we've got to do to receive it, is believe it. You can be saved right now by simply believing the Gospel. To summarize, in simple form that anybody can understand, here is what you must believe: That Jesus Christ was the Son of God, in human form, that He shed His blood on the Cross for remission of our sins, that He died on the Cross that we might have life, that He was buried and rose again the third day.

While you are believing, you might want to say the following "Salvation Prayer" to the Lord Jesus:

SALVATION PRAYER

Lord Jesus, thank you for loving me and dying for me on the Cross. Your precious blood washes me clean of every sin. You are my Lord and Saviour, now and forever. I believe that you rose from the dead and that you are alive today. Because of Your finished work, I am now a beloved child of God and heaven is my home. I thank you that my body is the temple of God and you have sent the Holy Spirit to dwell in me. I thank you for the tremendous price You paid to buy me back and I now am not my own, but belong to You. Thank you for giving me eternal life, and filling my heart with Your peace and joy. I love You, Lord Jesus. Amen.

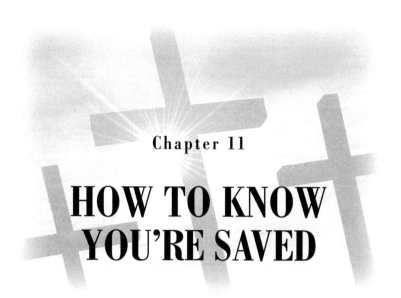

Chapter 11

HOW TO KNOW YOU'RE SAVED

You might ask, "How can I know that I'm a true believer?" "And not like a multitude of others who are simply church members and sitting in their pews for an hour on Sunday morning and hoping that they are okay." The following is the proof of your salvation:

First, make sure you understood and accepted Paul's Gospel of Salvation" believing that Jesus was the Son of God, that He died and shed His blood for the forgiveness of your sins, that He was buried, and that He was raised the third day. See I Corinthians 15:1-4.

Romans 8:16 At the moment you believe, the Holy Spirit will bear witness with your spirit, that you are a child of God. You will sense this and more likely than not, you will cry like a new-born babe (that's what you are: your spirit has been born again).

I Corinthians 2:14 *"But the natural* (unsaved) *man receiveth not the things of the Spirit of God: for they are*

foolishness (not able to be understood) ***unto him: neither can he know them, because they are spiritually discerned.***"

You will have a hunger for the Word of God. It follows, like daylight following darkness, that when we become a child of God, we will hunger for His Word. To you who have never been saved and to you who think you're saved but are not sure: remember how ever so often you read God's Word in a tract form or even the Bible and you couldn't understand one whit of It? It is not until you are truly saved that the Holy Spirit indwells you and enlightens the Word of God to you. The Holy Spirit was the divine author of the Book. He should be the best interpreter of the Book.

I might add, that your study of the Word, be limited, with few exceptions, to Paul's epistles, especially in the first stages of your Christian growth.

Hebrews 10:25a "Not forsaking the assembling of ourselves together..."

You will want to congregate and fellowship with others of like kindred (fellow believers) to comfort yourselves together, and edify and exhort one another.

It is important that we realize God loved us so much, He gave His Son to suffer and die for us. We will think on this love and all that Jesus accomplished on the Cross, not only at the time of salvation, but also during our entire Christian life.

Ephesians 5:20 "Giving thanks always for all things unto God and the Father in the name of our Lord Jesus Christ."

When saved, you will enjoy thanking and praising God continually for what He has done. When we study His Word and discover all that Jesus did for us, and what the indwelling Holy Spirit has done and is doing for us, our love for God will be magnified.

Psalms 34:1 "I will bless the Lord at all times: his praise shall continually be in my mouth."

The Holy Spirit will give you a boldness, power, and a desire to witness to others of the wondrous works of your Lord and Saviour. It will flow out as naturally as you breathe. The top priority and primary mission of every Christian is to be a soul winner. Solomon assured us that "he who wins souls is wise." (Proverbs 11:30)

II Corinthians 5:17 "Therefore if any man be in Christ, he is a new creature: old things are passed away; behold, all things are become new."

The things you once loved, you will now hate and the things you once hated, you will now love.

Immediately upon salvation, and later on as we grow in grace and mature as Christians, we will learn how to depend on the Holy Spirit and to allow Him to lead, direct, and guide our lives.

A Christian will have compassion on the poor and the needy; and will help them as he is able.

A Christian will communicate with the Lord often; much in tongues. Speaking in tongues will edify you (build you up).

As a Christian, you will forgive others, even as God for Christ's sake hath forgiven you (Ephesians 4:32).

Most, if not all of the above evidences of salvation, should exist immediately in the heart and life of a new-born Christian. Many other things came to us through the Cross and by the indwelling of the Holy Spirit, and they will become evident in our lives as we grow in grace and mature as Christians. For some of these things, see Chapters "What Happens When We're Saved", "Works of the Holy Spirit", "How to Witness", "Keys to Understanding the Bible", "Tongues", "Prayer", "Christian Growth", and "Reasons for Assembling With Other Believers – Local Church". Better yet, read this entire book. Above all, stay in the Word.

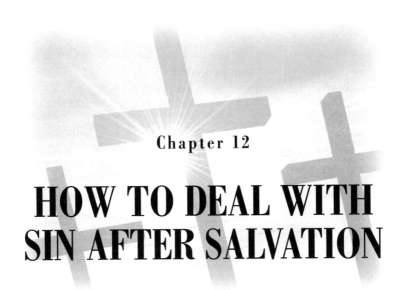

Chapter 12

HOW TO DEAL WITH SIN AFTER SALVATION

The Ten Commandments were never given to stop sin. They have no power to stop sin. God gave the law to expose man's sin. Today people are under the impression that if you preach strong and hard about the law, about all the "thou shalt nots", believers would be free from sin. Teaching the Ten Commandments will not stop sin, nor bring holiness. In fact, the law does just the opposite; it brings condemnation and death.

Colossians 2:14,15 *"Blotting out the handwriting of ordinances* (law) *that was against us, which was contrary to us, and took it out of the way, nailing it to the cross; And having spoiled principalities and powers, he made a shew of them openly, triumphing over them in it."*

When all the laws of the old covenant were nailed to the Cross of Jesus, the enemy and all his minions were disarmed. The devil can no longer use the law to condemn the believer, because the believer in Christ is free from the law. Even when you fail, the blood of Christ makes you righteous, just, and good. You are perfected by His grace in your life.

As long as you are in your present body, even after salvation, you will experience temptations, sinful desires, and sinful thoughts. The solution to these temptations, sinful desires, and sinful thoughts is found in **Romans 8:1a** *"There is therefore now no condemnation for those who are in Christ Jesus,..."* Notice that this verse is in the present tense. It is vitally important for you to receive the gift of "no condemnation" because that is what will give you the power to overcome your weaknesses, destructive habits and addictions.

Sin cannot take root in a believer who is full of consciousness that he is righteous in Christ. You cannot stop temptation and sinful thoughts and desires from coming into your mind, but you can certainly stop yourself from dwelling on and acting on them. How? By confessing at the very moment of temptation that you are the righteousness of God in Christ Jesus.

Romans 6:14 says that *"sin shall not have dominion over you, for you are not under the law but under grace."* When you know that Christ has made you righteous apart from your works, and that He has perfected you by His grace, that will give you the ability to overcome every sinful temptation, habit and addiction in your life. From the moment you accept Jesus as your personal Lord and Saviour, God sees you as perfect in His Son, the risen Christ, seated at His right hand. He does not condemn you for your past, present, and even your future mistakes because all the mistakes that you will make in this life have already been nailed to the Cross. As Jesus is spotless, and without blame, so are you! You are now free to sin no more, and experience victory and success over every sin and bondage in your life.

Once you accept Jesus as your personal Lord and Saviour, you are no longer a sinner. His perfect payment on the Cross cleared your lifetime of sin.

Before we obeyed from the heart that doctrine by which we are saved, we were the servants of sin unto death. Jesus, on the Cross bought us unto Himself out of Satan's slave market. Once we have come into the Grace of God and have comprehended all that God has done for us, how can we help but want to live with Him and serve Him. If thereafter, we continually dwell and act on temptations, sinful desires, and sinful thoughts; and desire to go back into the world, from which we were brought out of, we did not really understand the benefits Jesus provided for us on the Cross, or we did not truly believe with our whole heart; hence we are not saved.

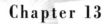

Chapter 13

CAN A TRUE CHRISTIAN FALL FROM GRACE

Are you one of those people who feel that you can not be assured of your grace? Do you hope to make it? Do you work like the dickens to hang on? Do you have to be sure that you don't sin in such a way that you will lose your salvation, and end up in Hell rather than God's Heaven?

Romans 8:35 "Who shall separate us from the love of Christ? shall tribulation or distress, or persecution, or famine, or nakedness, or peril, or sword?"

We may not be spared any of these things; in fact, more may come upon us than on the unsaved. Can the devil bring in enough persecution to force a believer out of his place in the Body of Christ? Never! When you are saved (believing on what Christ did on the Cross), the Holy Spirit baptizes you (places you) in the Body of Christ and you are there forever. If you were not sincere in your believing, the Holy Spirit, knowing your heart, did not place you in the Body of Christ. God has guaranteed that because of the work of the Cross, we are secure in Him. Not because of who we are, what we have done, or what we merit; but only because of what He has done.

Romans 8:38,39 "For I am persuaded, that neither death, nor life, nor angels, nor principalities, nor powers, nor things present, nor things to come, Nor height, nor depth, nor any other creature, shall be able to separate us from the love of God, which is in Christ Jesus, our Lord."

John 6:37 "All that the Father giveth me (those who get saved) ***shall come to me; and him that cometh to me I will in no wise cast out."***

John 10:27-29 "My sheep hear my voice, and I know them, and they follow me: And I give unto them eternal life; and they shall never perish, neither shall any man pluck them out of my hand. My Father, which gave them me, is greater than all; and no man is able to pluck them out of my Father's hand."

Ephesians 1:13,14 At salvation, we are sealed with that Holy Spirit of promise. That means our salvation is authenticated and no one or nothing can change it.

Romans 8:33 "Who shall lay any thing to the charge of God's elect? It is God that justifieth."

If we have been "truly saved", we belong to God. He has bought us with a price (His death). No one can take us out of His hand.

I John 2:1 *"My little children, these things I write unto you, that ye sin not. And if any man sin* (we're going to), *we have an advocate* (one who pleads our case) *with the Father, Jesus Christ the righteous."*

Satan accuses us before the Father. Jesus defends us by saying to the Father, "This son is considered righteous because he believed on Me and what I did on the Cross." Then the Father sees us as righteous through the blood of His Son.

Romans 8:1a *"There is therefore now no condemnation to them which are in Christ Jesus,..."*

Hebrews 13:5b *"...I will never leave thee nor forsake thee."*

Romans 8:14 *"For as many as are led by the Spirit of God, they are the sons of God."*

Romans 8:16 *"The Spirit itself beareth witness with our spirit, that we are the children of God."*

If you are a child of God, you will always be a child of God. We may think that God should kick someone out of His family, but the Scripture stands: If that person has genuinely entered in, he is in permanently. If you have gone through some set of rules whereby you became a church member, and automatically by rote repetition are qualified as a Christian, I don't buy that. People who simply walk the aisle, following whatever procedure may be given to them, and doing it by repetition are not <u>genuinely</u> saved. Today, we are in the Dispensation of Grace, not Law. The <u>only</u> means of salvation is Paul's Gospel; believing with all of our heart on what Christ did on the Cross. He died, shed His blood, was buried, and rose again the third day. (I Corinthians 15:1-4).

Chapter 14

WHAT HAPPENS WHEN WE'RE SAVED

We are saved. We are reconciled (brought back into fellowship) with God. ***Romans 5:10 "For if, when we were enemies, we were reconciled to God by the death of his Son, much more, being reconciled, we shall be saved by his Life."***

We are redeemed; our sins are forgiven. ***Colossians 1:14 "In whom we have redemption through his blood, even the forgiveness of sins:"***

The love of God is shed abroad in our hearts. ***Romans 5:5 "And hope maketh not ashamed, because the love of God is shed abroad in our hearts by the Holy Ghost which is given to us."***

We are delivered from the power of darkness and are translated into the kingdom of His dear Son. ***Colossians 1:13 "Who*** *hath delivered us from the power of darkness, and hath translated us into the kingdom of his dear Son:"*

Ephesians 1:13b "...in whom also after that ye believed, ye were sealed with that Holy Spirit of promise,"

We are the children of God. *Romans 8:16 "The Spirit itself beareth witness with our spirit, that we are the children of God;" Galatians 3:26 "For ye are all the children of God by faith in Christ Jesus."*

We are the sons of God. *Romans 8:14 "For as many as are led by the Spirit of God, they are the sons of God."*

We are justified. *Romans 3:24 "Being justified freely by his grace through the redemption that is in Christ Jesus:"*

We are heirs, heirs of God, and jointheirs with Christ. We are glorified. *Romans 8:17 "And if children, then heirs, heirs of God, and jointheirs with Christ; if so be that we suffer with him, that we may be also glorified together."*

Jesus is the propitiation for our sins. *Romans 3:25 "Whom God hath set forth to be a propitiation through faith in his blood, to declare his righteousness for the remission of sins that are past, through the forebearance of God;"*

We have peace with God. *Romans 5:1 "Therefore being justified by faith, we have peace with God through our Lord Jesus Christ:"*

Ephesians 2:13 "But now in Christ Jesus ye who sometimes were far off are made nigh by the blood of Christ."

We are made righteous. ***Romans 4:24*** *"But for us also, to whom it* (righteousness) *shall be imputed, if we believe on him that raised up Jesus our Lord from the dead;"* ***II Corinthians 5:21*** *"For he hath made him to be sin for us, who knew no sin; that we might be made the righteousness of God in Him."*

We have eternal life. ***Romans 5:21*** *"That as sin hath reigned unto death, even so might grace reign through righteousness unto eternal life by Jesus Christ our Lord."* ***Romans 6:23b*** *"...but the gift of God is eternal life through Jesus Christ our Lord."*

We died with Christ. ***Romans 6:3*** *"Know ye not, that so many of us as were baptized into* (placed into the Body of) *Jesus Christ were baptized into his death?"*

We are buried with Christ and are raised to newness of life. ***Romans 6:4,5*** *"Therefore we are buried with him by baptism into death: that like as Christ was raised up from the dead by the glory of the Father, even so we also should walk in newness of life. For if we have been planted together in the likeness of his death, we shall be also in the likeness of his resurrection."*

We are crucified (put to death) with Jesus. ***Romans 6:6*** *"Knowing this, that our old man is crucified with him, that the body of sin might be destroyed, that henceforth we should not serve sin."* ***Galatians 2:20*** *"I am crucified with Christ: nevertheless I live; yet not I, but Christ liveth in me: and the life which I now live in the flesh, I live by* *the faith of the Son of God who loved me, and gave Himself for me."*

We are freed from sin. **Romans 6:7** *"For he that is dead* (been crucified) *is freed from sin* (old Adam).*"*

We are redeemed from the curse of the law. **Galatians 3:13** *"Christ has redeemed us from the curse of the law, being made a curse for us: for it is written, Cursed is everyone that hangeth on a tree:"*

We shall live with Christ. **Romans 6:8** *"That if we be dead with Christ, we believe that we shall also live with him:"*

Sin hath no more dominion over us. **Romans 6:14** *"For sin shall not have dominion over you; for ye are not under the law, but under grace."*

We are made free from sin. **Romans 6:18a** *"Being then made free from sin..."* **Romans 6:22a** *"But now being made free from sin,..."*

We are become dead to the law. **Romans 7:4a** *"Wherefore, my brethren, ye also are become dead to the law by the body of Christ,..."*

We are married to Christ. **Romans 7:4b** *"...that ye should be married to another; even to him who is raised from the dead, that we should bring forth fruit unto God."* As God expects the fruit of a physical marriage to be children, so also the fruit of believers (Bride of Christ) shall be other believers.

We are delivered from the law. ***Romans 7:6*** *"But now we are delivered from the law, that being dead wherein we were held; that we should serve in newness of spirit, and not in the oldness of the letter."*

There is no condemnation to us. ***Romans 8:1*** *"There is therefore now no condemnation to them which are in Christ Jesus, who walk not after the flesh, but after the Spirit."*

We are not in the flesh. ***Romans 8:9*** *"But ye are not in the flesh, but in the Spirit, if so be that the Spirit of God dwell in you. Now if any man have not the Spirit of Christ, he is none of his."* It says in Romans, Chapter 8, the carnal mind is enmity against God, so then they that are in the flesh cannot please God. But God sending His own Son in the likeness of sinful flesh, and for sin, condemned sin in the flesh.

Galatians 5:24 *"And they that are Christ's have crucified* (put to death) *the flesh with the affections and lusts."*

He freely gives us all things. ***Romans 8:32*** *"He that spared not his own Son, but delivered him up for us all, how shall he not with him also freely give us all things?"*

We have fellowship with Jesus Christ our Lord. ***I Corinthians 1:9*** *"God is faithful, by whom ye were called unto the fellowship of His Son Jesus Christ our Lord."*

We have the power and wisdom of God. ***I Corinthians 1:24*** *"But unto them which are called, both Jews and Greeks, Christ the power of God, and the wisdom of God."*

We are sanctified. *I Corinthians 1:30 "But of him are you in Christ Jesus, who of God is made unto us wisdom, and righteousness, and sanctification, and redemption:"*

We are the temple of God. *I Corinthians 3:16 "Know ye not that ye are the temple of God, and that the Spirit of God dwelleth in you?" I Corinthians 6:19,20 "What? Know ye not that your body is the temple of the Holy Ghost which is in you, which ye have of God, and ye are not your own? For ye are bought with a price; therefore glorify God in your body, and in your spirit, which are God's."*

We are reconciled to God. *II Corinthians 5:18 "And all things are of God, who hath reconciled us to himself by Jesus Christ, and hath given to us the ministry of reconciliation;" Colossians 1:21 "And you, that were sometimes alienated and enemies in your mind by wicked works, yet now hath He reconciled."*

We do not fear. *II Timothy 1:7 "For God hath not given us the spirit of fear; but of power, and of love, and a sound mind."*

We are conquerors. *Romans 8:37 "Nay, in all things* (tribulation, distress, persecution, famine, nakedness, peril, or sword) *we are more than conquerors through Him that loved us."*

We are a new creature. *II Corinthians 5:17 "If any man be in Christ, he is a new creature: old things are passed away; behold all things become new."*

We are ambassadors for Christ. ***II Corinthians 5:20a "Now then we are ambassadors for Christ, as though God did beseech you by us;..."***

We have received the atonement. ***Romans 5:11 "And not only so, but we also joy in God through our Lord Jesus Christ, by whom we have now received the atonement."***

We are baptized (placed) unto one body. ***I Corinthians 12:13 "For by one Spirit are we all baptized into one body, whether we be Jews or Gentiles, whether we be bond or free, and have been all made to drink into one Spirit."***

God has set us in the Body. ***I Corinthians 12:18 "But now hath God set the members, everyone of them in the body, as it hath pleased him."***

We are the Body of Christ. ***I Corinthians 12:27 "Now ye are the body of Christ, and members in particular."***

Christ is the Head of the Body. ***Ephesians 1:22,23 "And hath put all things under his feet, and gave him to be the head over all things to the church, which is his body, the fulness of him that filleth all in all."***

Heaven is our home. ***Philippians 3:20a "For our conversation*** (citizenship) ***is in heaven;"***

See Chapter "Works of the Holy Spirit" for other Holy Spirit happenings that take place during our Christian growth, up to and including the Rapture.

It may seem as if you need to take a lot of action to have some of the above take place in your life; but not so. They are automatic and take place the moment you are saved. Immediately after salvation you are a babe in Christ and probably won't comprehend most of them. Just stay in the Word of God and one by one they will become part of you and will strengthen you in your Christian walk.

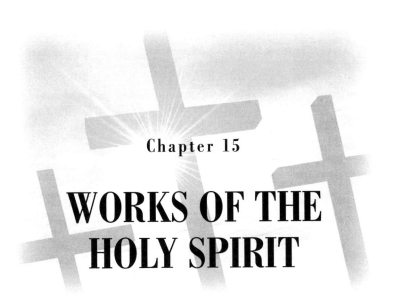

Chapter 15

WORKS OF THE HOLY SPIRIT

Holy men of God wrote the Bible, as they were moved upon by the inspiration or revelation of the Holy Spirit of God.

The Holy Spirit has always been the omnipresence of God on the planet. Back in Genesis 1:2, He moved upon the face of the waters.

Believers were not indwelt by the Holy Spirit in the Old Testament. The Spirit would come upon some, but He wasn't there permanently. Several in the New Testament were filled with the Spirit such as John the Baptist, his parents, Stephen, etc. The 120 disciples on the Day of Pentecost were filled with the Spirit in fulfillment of what the prophets of old had prophesied, and what Jesus had promised. They were to receive power to witness to the whole world – but they never did. That will happen during the Tribulation by the 144,000 young Jewish men.

I believe the Holy Spirit protects us from time of conception. I don't know of any scripture to substantiate this, but considering without God's protection, the fact that Satan came to steal, kill, and destroy, we wouldn't last two minutes, let alone long enough to receive salvation.

In this day and age, the Age of Grace, the Holy Spirit's main purpose is to glorify Jesus Christ (John 16:14). As the Son spent His entire life seeking to glorify the Father, the Holy Spirit spends His time seeking to glorify the Son. One way He does this is when we speak in "tongues", we allow the Holy Spirit (through us) to give praise unto the Lord Jesus Christ.

The particular work of the Holy Spirit is to impart life. It was so in Creation. It was so when He raised Jesus from the dead. It is so in the new birth.

It is the Holy Spirit Who accomplishes the will of God for the Christian. First, conviction; that operation of the Holy Spirit by which the sinner is made to feel his lost condition (because of sin) and his need for a Saviour. This is important because man will never take the initiative in coming to God. Jesus Himself said, "No man can come to Me, except the Father Which hath sent Me, draw him." Through the Holy Spirit, God draws men to Himself. Secondly, the god of this world (Satan) hath blinded the minds of them which believe not (II Corinthians 4:3,4). But the Holy Spirit supercedes this blindness and gives the unbeliever a clear mind and a receptive heart to desire salvation. A third thing the Holy Spirit does for the unbeliever is to give him the measure of faith (Romans 12:3b), faith sufficient to believe for salvation. This has to be; otherwise, man could never be saved. Believing is required for salvation. Believing (faith) cometh by hearing (Romans

10:17). Unsaved man can't hear because the Gospel is foolishness (not understood) to him. It is foolishness because he does not have the Holy Spirit to enlighten it to him (I Corinthians 2:14), and lastly, he does not have the Holy Spirit because he is not saved (Romans 8:9). I believe the only time God gives us the necessary faith is when He gives us the faith required to believe for salvation. After salvation, to receive anything from God, the faith required will have to come by hearing the Word.

The moment we are saved, God sends the Holy Spirit to indwell us (I Corinthians 3:16).

Romans 8:16 "The Spirit itself beareth witness with our spirit, that we are the children of God."

The Holy Spirit gives us a boldness, power, and desire to witness to the unsaved. Witnessing is the primary mission of every Christian.

I Corinthians 2:12 "Now we have received, not the spirit of the world, but the Spirit which is of God; that we might know the things that are freely given to us of God."

As soon as we believe the Gospel, the "Word of God" begins to open up to our understanding.

The Holy Spirit "testifies" of Jesus.

The Holy Spirit makes Christ real to us in His full, unlimited, invisible Self.

The Holy Spirit empowers us with "power from on high."

The Holy Spirit will guide us into all truth and show us things to come (John 16:13).

The Holy Spirit, that is in us, is greater than the devil, who is in the world.

We are conquerors. **Romans 8:37** *"Nay, in all things* (tribulation, distress, persecution, famine, nakedness, peril or sword) *we are more than conquerors through him that loved us."*

We can resist the devil through the power of the Holy Spirit, and Satan has to flee.

John 14:26 "But the Comforter, which is the Holy Spirit, whom the Father will send in my name, He shall teach you all things, and bring all things to your remembrance, whatsoever I have said unto you."

We are saved from the wrath of God. **Romans 5:9** *"Much more then, being now justified by his blood, we shall be saved from wrath* (the Tribulation) *through him."*

I Corinthians 2:9,10 "But, as it is written, Eye hath not seen, nor ear heard, neither hath entered into the heart of man, the things which God hath prepared for them that love him. But God hath revealed them unto us by his Spirit; for the Spirit searcheth all things, yea, the deep things of God."

We are raised to newness of life. **Romans 6:4b,5** *"...that, like as Christ was raised up from the dead by the glory of the Father, even so we also should walk in newness of life.*

For if we have been planted together in the likeness of his death, we shall be also in the likeness of his resurrection:"

We shall live with Christ. **Romans 6:8** *"Now if we be dead with Christ, we believe that we shall also live with him:"*

Romans 8:27 *"And he that searcheth the hearts knoweth what is the mind of the Spirit, because he maketh intercession for the saints according to the will of God."*

Romans 8:26 *"Likewise the Spirit also helpeth our infirmitives* (our weaknesses); *for we know not what we should pray for as we ought: but the Spirit Itself maketh intercession for us with groanings which cannot be uttered."* This is speaking in "tongues".

When we pray in the Spirit, the Holy Spirit may pray to God about things, people, or situations that we know not of. And remember, when we "speak in tongues" we edify ourselves.

Galatians 5:22,23 *"But the fruit of the Spirit is love, joy, peace, longsuffering, gentleness, goodness, faith, meekness, temperance: against such things there is no law."*

See Chapter "What Happens When We're Saved" for a list of other Holy Spirit happenings which take place in our lives immediately upon receiving salvation.

Chapter 16

MYSTERIES

A mystery in Scripture is a thing which has been kept secret, in the heart of God, from the foundation of the world, until He revealed it to man. It is something that human reasoning could never discover.

Following are eight mysteries that were revealed to the Apostle Paul before anyone else: Israel's Blindness; The Rapture; God's Will; Godliness; Christ; Christ in us; The Body of Christ, the Church, the Bride; and Iniquity.

One of the mysteries given to Paul was that <u>BLINDNESS in part has happened to Israel</u> (Romans 11:25). This period of blindness is from the time Paul started preaching his gospel of salvation until the fulness of the Gentiles be come in. This period of time began about 0040 AD when the believers at Antioch were first called Christians, and will end when the last member of the Body of Christ has been added. This completes the Church and the Church will be raptured. The Bible says there is a remnant of Jews who will be saved by Paul's Gospel and the rest will be blinded.

Because of their unbelief Israel stumbled and fell, and through their fall, salvation came unto the Gentiles. Some of the branches of the natural olive tree were broken off, and we, being a wild olive tree are grafted in by faith.

Romans 11:26a says, "And all Israel shall be saved:..." This will happen at the end of the Tribulation when Christ returns to the earth and the Jews will accept Him as their Messiah. The "all" pertains to the ones remaining at the time of Christ's return. Most will have lost their lives during the Tribulation.

Another mystery given to Paul is the "RAPTURE". We shall not all sleep, but we shall all be changed (I Corinthians 15:51). The event spoken of here is commonly referred to as the "Rapture of the Church". This event will occur at the end of the "Church Age", the "Age of Grace", when the last member is added to the Body of Christ. All those, and only those, who are saved by Paul's Gospel and what God has said concerning the finished work of the Cross, will be involved. The dead in Christ will rise first and then we who are alive physically will rise to meet Jesus in the air, and we will be forever with Him. See Chapter, "The Rapture".

Another mystery – mystery of "GOD'S WILL".

Ephesians 1:9 "Having made known unto us the mystery of his will, according to his good pleasure which he hath purposed in himself:"

Galatians 1:4 *"Who* (the Lord Jesus Christ) *gave himself for our sins, that he might deliver us from this present evil world, according to the will of God and our Father:"*

I Timothy 2:4 *"It is God's will for all men to be saved, and come unto the knowledge of the truth."*

II Peter 3:9b *"...The Lord is not willing that any should perish, but that all should come to repentance."*

Ephesians 1:10 *"That in the dispensation of the fulness of times he might gather together in one all things in Christ, both which are in heaven, and which are on earth; even in him."*

Ephesians 1:4,5 *"According as he hath chosen us in him before the foundation of the world, that we should be holy and without blame before him in love: Having predestinated us unto the adoption of children by Jesus Christ to himself, according to the good pleasure of his will,"*

Ephesians 1:11 *"In whom also we have obtained an inheritance, being predestinated according to the purpose of him who worketh all things after the counsel of his own will:"*

By the will of Christ, He did away with the sacrifices required by the law and established the sacrifice of His own body once for all (Hebrews 10:8-10).

Mystery of GODLINESS

I Timothy 3:16 *"And without controversy great is the mystery of Godliness: God was manifest in the flesh, justified in the Spirit, seen of angels, preached unto the Gentiles, believed on in the world, received up into glory."*

I Timothy 4:7 "But refuse profane and old wives' fables, and exercise thyself rather unto godliness."

I Timothy 4:8 "For bodily exercise profiteth little: but godliness is profitable unto all things, having promise of the life that now is, and of that which is to come."

I Timothy 4:10 "For therefore we both labour and suffer reproach; because we trust in the living God, who is the saviour of all men, specially of those that believe."

I Timothy 6:6 "But godliness with contentment is great gain."

Paul told Timothy to give attendance to reading, to exhortation, to doctrine.

<u>Mystery of CHRIST</u>

Colossians 1:15,16 "Jesus is the image of the invisible God, the firstborn of every creature: for by him were all things created, that are in heaven, and that are in earth, visible and invisible, whether they be thrones, dominions, or principalities, or powers: all things were created by him and for him:"

Colossians 1:17 "And he is before all things, and by him all things consist."

Colossians 2:9 "For in him dwelleth all the fulness of the Godhead bodily."

Hebrews 9:11a "But Christ being come an high priest of good things to come,..."

Hebrews 7:24 "But this man, because he continueth ever, hath an unchangeable priesthood."

Hebrews 4:14a "Seeing then that we have a great high priest, that is passed into the heavens; Jesus the son of God,..."

Hebrews 9:24 "For Christ is not entered into the holy places made with hands, which are figures of the true, but into heaven itself, now to appear in the presence of God for us:"

Hebrews 9:12 "Neither by the blood of goats and calves, but by his own blood he entered in once into the holy place, having obtained eternal redemption for us."

Hebrews 10:12 "But this man, after he had offered one sacrifice for sins for ever, sat down on the right hand of God;"

Hebrews 10:14 "For by one offering he hath perfected for ever them that are sanctified."

God wants us, who believe, to know the greatness of His power which He wrought in Christ, when He raised Him from the dead (Ephesians 1:19,20).

Colossians 1:20a "And, having made peace through the blood of the Cross, by him to reconcile all things unto himself,..."

Colossians 1:18a "And he is the head of the body, the church:..."

Ephesians 1:22,23 "God the Father hath put all things under Jesus' feet, and gave him to be the head over all things to the church, Which is his body, the fulness of him that filleth all in all."

<u>Mystery of CHRIST IN US</u>

Colossians 1:27 "To whom God would make known what is the riches of the glory of this mystery among the Gentiles: which is Christ in you, the hope of glory:"

God has chosen us in Him (Christ) before the foundation of the world, that we should be holy and without blame before Him in love (Ephesians 1:4): God the Father hath put all things under Jesus' feet, and gave Him to be the Head over all things to the Church, which is His Body, the fulness of Him that filleth all in all (Ephesians 1:22,23). But God, Who is rich in mercy, for His great love wherewith He loved us, even when we were dead in sins, has made us alive together with Christ (by grace ye are saved, not of yourselves, it is the gift of God, not of works, lest any man should boast) and has raised us up together, and made us sit together in heavenly places in Christ Jesus (Ephesians 2:4-9):

Ephesians 1:7 "In whom we have redemption through his blood, the forgiveness of sins, according to the riches of his grace;"

After that we believed the gospel of salvation, we are sealed with the Holy Spirit of promise (Ephesians 1:13). We are sealed unto the day of redemption (Ephesians 4:30).

II Corinthians 5:17 "If any man be in Christ, he is a new creature; old things are passed away; behold, all things are become new."

Ephesians 4:22-24 "That ye put off concerning the former conversation (way of life) *the old man which is corrupt according to the deceitful lusts; And be renewed in the spirit of your mind; And that ye put on the new man which after God is created in righteousness and true holiness."*

We can expect the Father of glory to give unto us the spirit of wisdom and revelation in the knowledge of Him (Ephesians 1:17): and that the eyes of our understanding will be enlightened; that we may know what is the hope of His calling, and what the riches of the glory of His inheritance in the saints, and what is the exceeding greatness of His power to us-ward who believe, according to the working of His mighty power, which He wrought in Christ, when He raised Him from the dead, and set Him at His own right hand in the heavenly places (Ephesians 1:18-20).

Ephesians 3:6 "That the Gentiles, (through faith in Christ) *should be fellow heirs, and of the same body, and partakers of His promise in Christ by the gospel."*

That we might know the manifold wisdom of God (Ephesians 3:10). That we according to the riches of His glory, be strengthened with might by His Spirit in the inner man (Ephesians 3:16); that we might be rooted and grounded in love (Ephesians 3:17); that we may know the love of Christ, which passeth knowledge; that we might be filled with all the fulness of God (Ephesians 3:19).

Now, glory be unto Him that is able to do exceeding abundantly above all that we ask or think, according to the power that worketh in us (Ephesians 3:20).

Colossians 2:10 *"We are complete in Him* (Jesus), *which is the head of all principality and power:"*

By the circumcision of Christ, the sins of the flesh have been put off the body (Colossians 2:11). We are buried with Christ in baptism and are risen to new life, through the faith of the operation of God, Who hath raised Him from the dead (Colossians 2:12). We, being dead in our sins and the uncircumcision of our flesh, hath He quickened (made alive) together with Him, having forgiven us all trespasses (Colossians 2:13). He blotted out the handwriting of ordinances (laws) that was against us, which was contrary to us, and took it out of the way, nailing it to His Cross (Colossians 2:14). We are dead (to sins), and our life is hid with Christ in God. When Christ, Who is our life, shall appear, then shall we also appear with Him in glory (Colossians 3:3,4). We are in Christ Jesus, Who of God is made unto us wisdom, and righteousness, and sanctification, and redemption (I Corinthians 1:30).

The Mystery of <u>THE BODY OF CHRIST, THE CHURCH, THE BRIDE</u>.

See Chapter on SAME.

<u>MYSTERY OF INIQUITY</u>,

(II Thessalonians 2:7,8a) *"For the mystery of iniquity doth already work: only he* (the Holy Spirit) *who now letteth* (hinders) *will let* (hinder), *until he* (the Holy Spirit) *be taken out of the way. And then shall that wicked* (the antichrist) *be revealed,..."*

II Thessalonians 2:9 *"Even him, whose coming is after the working of Satan with all power and signs and lying wonders."* The spiritual restraining power keeping antichrist from arising is the Holy Spirit residing in the hearts of believers, the Body of Christ. When the believers are raptured, then the antichrist is free to appear and the seven-year Tribulation period will begin.

Paul has revealed the "mystery of godliness" – God manifest in the flesh, Christ.

Paul, now reveals the "mystery of iniquity" – Satan manifest in the flesh, antichrist.

Chapter 17

THE BODY OF CHRIST, THE CHURCH, THE BRIDE

I Corinthians 12:12,13 *"For as the body is one, and hath many members, and all the members of that one body, being many, are one body: so also is Christ. For by one Spirit are we all baptized* (placed in the Body of Christ) *into one body, whether we be Jews or Gentiles, whether we be bond or free; and have been all made to drink into one Spirit."*

I Corinthians 12:14 *"For the body is not one member, but many."*

I Corinthians 12:27 *"Now ye are the body of Christ, and members in particular."*

I Corinthians 6:15a "Know ye not that your bodies are the members of Christ?..."

Today, many Christian groups require water baptism for membership. People are baptized, and become members, but are not saved. There will be no unbelievers in the Body of Christ because that's the work of the Holy Spirit to immediately place or baptize them into the Body of Christ. The Body of Christ is also referred to as "The Church" and "The Bride of Christ."

Romans 7:4 "Wherefore, my brethren, ye also are become dead to the law by the body of Christ (His physical body that was crucified); *that ye should be married to another, even to him who is raised from the dead, that we should bring forth fruit unto God."*

As Eve was taken from the side of Adam, so the Church is taken out of the pierced side of our Lord Jesus Christ. The Church is born out of His blood, His sufferings, and His Cross. The first Adam had a bride – Eve. The Second Adam has a bride – the Church. Just as God expected Adam and Eve to replenish the earth, He expects the Church to bring forth fruit (other believers) unto Him.

Ephesians 5:25b,26,27 "...even as Christ also loved the Church, and gave himself for it; That he might sanctify and cleanse it with the washing of water by the word, That he might present it to himself a glorious church, not having spot, or wrinkle, or any such thing: but that it should be holy and without blemish."

Jesus is the Saviour of the Body, the Head of the Church, and the Husband of the Bride (Ephesians, Chapter 5). The Church, the Body, and the Bride are all one and the same. Jesus expects them all to be holy and without spot, wrinkle, or blemish. Do you think He is going to take any Tom, Dick or Harry as His Bride or His Body? I think not. He is going to take only those who have believed in that which He provided on the Cross. The only way you're going to be without spot or wrinkle is to be saved by the Gospel of Grace, during the Age of Grace. At the time of salvation, we put on the new man, which after God is created in righteousness and true holiness (Ephesians 4:24).

This period, the Age of Grace, started with the saving of the first Christian at the church in Antioch, about ten years after Pentecost (Acts, Chapter 11), and will end at the time of the Rapture. Those saved outside of this time period will have a different position in Christ in eternity.

***Colossians 1:18** "And he is the head of the body, the church: Who is the beginning, the first-born from the dead; that in all things he might have preeminence."*

When Jesus was on earth, He Himself was the Body of Christ. Now the Holy Spirit indwells believers and THEY become Christ's Body, the Church.

***Colossians 1:24** "Who now rejoice in my sufferings for you, and fill up that which is behind of the afflictions of Christ in my flesh for his body's sake, which is the church:"*

***Romans 11:25** "For I would not, brethren, that ye should be ignorant of this mystery* (secret)*, lest ye should* *be wise in your own conceits; that blindness* (a spiritual blindness) *in part* (one day this blindness will end) *is happened to Israel, until the fulness of the Gentiles be come in.*"

Now what's the fulness of the Gentiles? When the Body of Christ is complete. When the last believer (of Paul's Gospel) is baptized (placed) into the Body of Christ, the Rapture will occur and God will pick up where He left off with the Nation of Israel, with another Gospel.

Chapter 18

CHRISTIAN GROWTH

Salvation is an instantaneous, one time event. Christian growth and Bible understanding are processes.

When we were first saved, we acknowledged what Christ did for us on the Cross, but it's important to realize and consider daily how much Jesus loves us. It is also important to know that the Holy Spirit indwells us; to know what He did for us at salvation, and to know what He can do and will do for us after salvation. Some of these things depend on, not only our knowing, but whether or not we will allow or depend upon Him doing. See Chapters "What Happens When We're Saved" and "Works of the Holy Spirit".

First thing, speak in tongues: this can happen immediately upon receiving salvation. Speaking in tongues edifies (builds up) our spirit. The Holy Spirit helps our infirmities (weaknesses) in that He prays through us for things we know not of.

Naturally we are to grow in grace. We are to grow in the knowledge of the Word. We are to grow in our works and our activities for the Lord's business. Every believer has at least one gift that can be used in God's service: pray, sing, teach, witness, preach, play instrument, give, minister to the poor and the sick, etc. Absolutely we're to help the needy and the poor, to be cheerful givers, and to be witnesses, and that is why we're left here. II Corinthians 5:20a tells us that we are ambassadors for Christ. Our message to the world should be Jesus and Him Crucified.

II Corinthians 6:14 "Be ye not unequally yoked together with unbelievers, for what fellowship hath righteousness with unrighteousness? And what communion hath light with darkness?"

You definitely will want to obey this scripture if you get married after you are saved. Also, you will probably have to revise your list of friends, since an unsaved person will drag you down and hinder your spiritual growth.

As far as Bible understanding is concerned, let's start with FAITH.

II Corinthians 5:7 "(For we walk by faith, not by sight:)"

Remember, without faith it is impossible to please God. And faith cometh by hearing, and hearing by the Word of God. I've heard that one must hear something seven or more times before you really hear it and get it down in your heart. I think you'll agree with me that the Bible is harder to understand than other things we read, and we may have to read It many times to really hear It. You can't read the Bible like any other book. You've got to take

It one Word at a time. You've got to see who's speaking, who is being spoken to, what's spoken of, and the time frame.

Don't confuse Israel with the Church. The God of Israel in Genesis is the same God that we deal with today, but He deals with us, the Church, under far different circumstances.

You can gain knowledge of the Word by assembling yourself together with other believers and studying or you can study on your own. Either way, the Holy Spirit is a great help in enlightening the Word to you. He wrote the Bible. He is able to interpret it.

No one will ever understand all of the Bible, so don't get discouraged. You don't have to memorize scriptures, but you will some. When you need a certain scripture to stand on or to relate to someone you are witnessing to, the Holy Spirit will bring it to your remembrance.

There are books and TV preachings and presentations out there, but I wouldn't put much faith in them – most contain false teaching and false doctrine.

Until you become well-established as a believer, I would stick with Paul's epistles; Romans through Philemon. Then Hebrews, and the rest of the Bible, because all scripture is given by inspiration of God, and is profitable for doctrine, for instruction in righteousness, and It ties everything together.

I Corinthians 3:9 "For we are labourers together with God; ye are God's husbandry, ye are God's building."

Paul says we should be careful how we build (live our lives) on the foundation that is laid. For other foundation can no man lay than that is laid, which is Christ Jesus. All our works, after salvation, will be tried by fire. If our works survive the fire we will receive a reward. If our works are burned, we will suffer loss, but we ourselves shall be saved (I Corinthians 3:10-15). Everything we say or do should be pleasing to God.

To aid in our Christian growth, the following scripture verses are provided for our understanding and/or action:

(Psalms 34:1) Let praise continually be in your mouth.

(Psalms 34:19) Many are the afflictions of the righteous; but the Lord delivereth them out of them all.

(Proverbs 10:22) The blessing of the LORD, it maketh rich, and He addeth no sorrow with it.

(Proverbs 11:30b) He that winneth souls is wise.

(Romans 5:3,4) We glory in tribulation, knowing that tribulation worketh patience; and patience, experience; and experience, hope.

(Romans 12:9b) Abhor that which is evil; cleave to that which is good.

(Romans 12:12) Rejoicing in hope, patient in tribulation, continuing instant in prayer.

(Romans 12:17) Recompense to no man evil for evil. Provide things honest in the sight of all men.

(Romans 12:19) Avenge not yourselves; vengeance is mine; I will repay, saith the Lord.

(Romans 13:9b) Thou shalt love your neighbor as yourself.

(Romans 13:14) But put ye on the Lord Jesus Christ, and make not provision for the flesh, to fulfil the lusts thereof.

(Romans 14:1-3) Don't argue with or judge one who eats what you don't or who does not eat what you do.

(Romans 14:5) One man esteemeth one day (Sabbath, etc.) above another; another esteemeth every day alike. Let every man be fully persuaded in his own mind.

(Romans 14:13) Don't judge. Don't put a stumbling block or an occasion to fall in your brother's way.

(I Corinthians 10:13) There hath no temptation taken you but such as is common to man; but God is faithful; Who will not suffer you to be tempted above that you are able, but will with the temptation also make a way to escape, that ye may be able to bear it.

(II Corinthians 12:14b) The children ought not to lay up for the parents, but the parents for the children.

(Ephesians 4:30a) Grieve not the Holy Spirit of God.

(Ephesians 4:32b) Forgive one another, even as God for Christ's sake hath forgiven you.

(Philippians 3:20) For our conversation (whole tenor of our life, acts, and thoughts) is in heaven; from whence also we look for the Saviour, the Lord Jesus Christ.

(Philippians 4:11) Be content in whatsoever state you are.

(I Timothy 6:8) Having food and raiment, let us be therefore content.

(Hebrews 13:5) Be content with such things as ye have.

(Romans 8:28a) All things work together for good to them that love God.

(I Timothy 6:10a) For the love of money is the root of all evil.

(I Thessalonians 5:16) We should rejoice evermore.

(I Thessalonians 5:17) We should pray without ceasing.

(I Thessalonians 5:18) We should, in everything give thanks.

What the devil makes for harm, God makes for good.

Our "old" lives were nailed to the Cross with Jesus. By that we count ourselves DEAD to sin and ALIVE unto God.

We live in this world, but we are not of it. We have died with Christ to this world; we now live with Him on earth, but in "heavenly places" in the spirit.

Chapter 19

TONGUES

Tongues is speaking to God in the Spirit out of the depths of your inner-most being, your spirit. It is important to know that your spirit can communicate directly with God, without the aid of your mind.

I Corinthians 3:16 "Know ye not that ye are the temple of God, and that the Spirit of God dwelleth in you?"

In Christendom today, the indwelling of the Holy Spirit is not taught. People seek the "Infilling of the Holy Spirit", evidenced by "speaking in tongues", so they can "speak in tongues" and have "power to witness". In seeking, they are told to repeat certain words, tarry until, hang on, let go, yield, etc. They're spit on, slapped on, beat on the back, and I don't know what all. I can't find any of this stuff in my Bible.

When you are saved; I mean really saved by believing the Gospel of Christ; that He died, shed His blood, and rose again the third day, you are indwelt immediately by the Holy Spirit. How much of the Holy Spirit does it take for an individual to speak in tongues? The presence of the Holy Spirit in you at Salvation is all-sufficient, not only for you to speak in tongues, but for you to have a more abundant life. See Chapter "Works of the Holy Spirit".

Begging Jesus to fill you with His Spirit after you are saved is tantamount to confessing your sins and asking for forgiveness after Salvation, as if He didn't shed enough blood on the Cross to forgive your future sins.

When you speak in tongues, the Holy Spirit gives the power of utterance. It stands to reason, if you are not saved, you do not have the Holy Spirit and you cannot talk in tongues. In the same way a lot of people think they are saved and are not, I suspect their "speaking in tongues" can be attributed to the work of Satan. It is true he can work supernatural signs, counterfeits of God. Pertaining to salvation, the devil keeps them in the dark concerning scripture, answers just enough of their "prayers" to satisfy them, and make them think they're receiving from God, and keeps them comfortable in their "Christian" walk. Satan has "gotten" this world right where he wants it.

Immediately, upon being saved, you can "speak in tongues". All you have to do is raise your hands, close your eyes, place your thoughts totally upon what Jesus did on the Cross just for you, open your mouth and begin praising Jesus out loud, with sounds not in English or your own language. The Holy Spirit will take over and you are now "speaking in tongues".

There are two purposes for tongues: (1) As a personal private prayer language to God; (2) Separately, as a Gift of Tongues, which is one of the nine gifts of the Spirit.

Romans 8:26 *"Likewise the Spirit also helpeth our infirmities* (our weaknesses)*; for we know not what we should pray for as we ought; but the Spirit itself maketh intercession for us with groanings which cannot be uttered."*

Romans 8:27 *"And He that searcheth the hearts knoweth what is the mind of the Spirit, because He maketh intercession for the saints according to the will of God."*

When we pray in the Spirit, the Holy Spirit may pray to God about things, people, or situations that we know not of. But most of the time the Holy Spirit is giving praise and glory to Jesus Christ, magnifying the Son through us.

Jesus said in *John 16:13,14* *"When the Holy Spirit is come, He shall not speak of Himself; He shall glorify me."*

Our personal private prayer language can be used any time we will throughout our Christian life. This speaking in tongues, for the individual's benefit, edifies the individual's spirit, bringing spiritual release and inner therapy. I praise the Lord much each day. I start off in English and almost immediately tongues take over. I don't know why it makes us feel so good other than the Word says it will edify us (build us up).

Paul says in *I Corinthians 14:13* *"Wherefore, let him that speaketh in an unknown tongue, pray that he may interpret."*

Then, in a believer's personal prayer language, what is spoken in tongues is made understandable back to the believer.

The "Gift of Tongues" is not for yourself, but that which you are to manifest only in behalf of the needs of other Christians.

It is a special and separate manifestation of the Holy Spirit as He alone WILLS at a particular moment in a meeting or a group of believers.

In a meeting of believers where tongues are understood, the Holy Spirit may choose a time in the service when a Gift of Tongues will help, if interpreted; giving further edification (building up of the spirit) to other believers. At that time the TONGUE is followed by the Holy Spirit manifesting the Gift of Interpretation of Tongues, that Spirit-given ability given to the one who spoke in the Tongues Gift, or to another nearby, to interpret back to the minds of the believers, God's response.

The Gift of Prophecy, another Gift of the Spirit, is a horizontal form of speaking, from man to man, from one person to another. He that prophesieth speaketh unto men to edification and exhortation and comfort (I Corinthians 14:3). Tongues are not horizontal, but vertical; from man to God. And for tongues to be understandable to man, they have to be interpreted.

Interpretation is what makes the Gift of Tongues effective. Together, they are the equivalent of Prophecy.

Concerning Spiritual Gifts, Paul seemed to be more concerned with the edifying of the Church than anything else (I Corinthians 14:5,12).

The apostle Paul says when you come together and tongues and interpretations are in operation; let it be by two or at the most three. Also let the prophets speak two or three. Let all things be done decently and in order.

The church, today, bases everything they say or do concerning the infilling of the Holy Spirit with the evidence of speaking in tongues, on Acts, Chapter 2, and the day of Pentecost. This was the day of Pentecost. It was taking place in Jerusalem and it was a Jewish feast day. Those who were filled and those who were hearers of the gospel were Jews. Gentiles had nothing to with Pentecost; therefore, Acts 2 has nothing to do with us today.

Before His ascension to the Father, Jesus commanded the apostles to wait for the promise of the Father, which was the baptism of the Holy Ghost, by which they would receive power to be witnesses unto Jesus unto the world. When the day of Pentecost was come, the apostles and others were filled with the Holy Ghost and spake in tongues. The only criteria for receiving the Holy Ghost was to wait. This was because the Holy Spirit had not yet been given; because that Jesus was not yet glorified (John 7:39).

In *I Corinthians 14:2* Paul says, *"For he that speaketh in an unknown tongue speaketh not unto men, but unto God: for no man understandeth him; howbeit in the spirit he speaketh mysteries."*

But, I believe the speakers in Acts 2, speaking in "other" tongues were MIRACULOUSLY inspired for the purpose of preaching the Gospel of the Kingdom in the languages (OTHER) of the Jews who had come from nations of the world to celebrate the day of Pentecost. I think this was a one-time occurrence in that time. I think it may happen today, but not very often, that God would translate a missionary worker to some land and preach the Gospel to the people in their own language or tongue. Just remember, God is Sovereign.

Chapter 20

BAPTISM

There is no other subject in Christianity that causes more disagreement among the people than water baptism. They differ on the method: sprinkling, pouring water on, dipping, total immersion, etc. They differ on whose name it should be done in: the Name of Jesus or the Name of the Father, the Son, and the Holy Ghost. Sometimes there is argument over who should do the baptizing. And then there is the reason for being baptized. Some say it is to show the world that they have been saved. The world could care less. Some say it is a commandment of God or an ordinance to be kept. Some say that it is a memorial – a memorial to what, I don't know. Some are baptized because their pastor says it is the right thing to do. Some say they are led of the Lord to be baptized. Some churches require baptism as a prerequisite to joining the church. And then some say baptism is required for salvation. This is probably due to the fact that when Israel was delivered out of Egypt and was come into Sinai, God said in **Exodus 19:5,6a** *"Now therefore, if you will obey my voice indeed, and keep my covenant, then ye shall be a peculiar treasure unto me above all people: for all the* *earth is mine: And ye shall be unto me a kingdom of priests, and an holy nation."*

Before priests could perform their duties they had to wash, wash, and wash some more. The Jews experienced that symbolic washing with their baptism.

John the Baptist, forerunner of Jesus, preached "Repent and be baptized for the remission of sin, for the kingdom of heaven is at hand.

Jesus, after being baptized by John, preached the same: repent, for the kingdom of God is at hand. Why was Jesus baptized? He didn't have any sin to repent of. He came to be a prophet, priest, and King; and in order to fulfill all of the requirements of the priesthood again, He had to symbolically fulfill the washing at the baptism. In the Jordan, He did this and also identified Himself with His Covenant people, the Nation of Israel.

In Acts 2, the apostles received the baptism of the Holy Ghost for the purpose of receiving power to continue the teaching, healings, and miracle workings of Jesus to the world after He was crucified. They expected Jesus to come back and set up His Kingdom, but Jesus turned to the Gentiles with the Gospel of Grace, to call out a people for His name.

Now, let's see what the Bible says about spiritual baptism:

I Corinthians 3:16 "Know ye not that ye are the temple of God and that the Spirit of God dwells in you?"

At the moment a person believes for salvation by Paul's Gospel, God sends the Holy Spirit to indwell him and reside in him forever.

I Corinthians 12:13a *"For by one Spirit are we all baptized into one body,..."*

At the moment of salvation, the Holy Spirit baptizes us (places us) into the body of Christ, of which Christ is the Head. The "Body of Christ" is also called "The Church". There are no unbelievers in the Body of Christ, because only believers are placed there by the Holy Spirit.

Ephesians 4:4,5 *"There is one body* (The Body of Christ), *and one Spirit* (The Holy Spirit)*, even as ye are called in one hope of your calling; one Lord, one faith, one baptism,"*

Galatians 3:27 *"For as many of you as have been baptized into Christ have put on Christ."*

Romans 6:3 *"Know ye not, that so many of us as were baptized into Jesus Christ were baptized into His death?"*

So you see, the only baptisms we are concerned with today are those which the Holy Spirit performs. We do not choose. It is automatic, the moment we believe for salvation. Note that all scriptures concerning baptisms which are for us today are found in, and only in, Paul's epistles; and there is not one drop of water in any.

Chapter 21

PRAYER

Prayer is one of the highest functions, and one of the most important privileges of a Christian. To pray is as much a part of the Christian life as breathing is to the natural life.

Ephesians 5:20 "Giving thanks always for all things unto God and the Father in the name of our Lord Jesus Christ:"

Here and in other locations in the Scriptures, we are told that when we pray, we should pray to our Heavenly Father in the name of Jesus Christ. But, I don't think God will chastise us, if when we pray, we address any person of the Godhead, calling them Father, Jesus, or Holy Spirit.

I like to think of prayer as communicating with God, which may include worship, praise, adoration, thanksgiving, intercession for others, supplication, entreating (asking for, earnestly), etc. Also, there is the personal, private, prayer language (tongues) whereby the Holy Spirit intercedes for us. See Chapter "Tongues".

Philippians 4:6 "Be careful for nothing; but in every-thing by prayer and supplication (asking for humbly) *with thanksgiving let your requests be known unto God."*

I Thessalonians 5:17 "Pray without ceasing."

I Thessalonians 5:18 "In everything give thanks."

Psalms 34:1 "Let praise continually be in your mouth."

Upon awakening each morning, I like to ask the Holy Spirit to lead and direct my life that day and to schedule everything He wants me to do and say that day.

Personally, I don't spend a lot of time asking God to do something for myself. The apostle Paul, in Philippians, tells us to be content in whatsoever state we find ourselves. Also, in Hebrews, Paul instructs us to be content with such things as we have. In other words, we are not to be envious, greedy, or covetous. As earthly fathers provide for their children, how much more shall we, as God's children, receive from our Heavenly Father, our needs without us asking.

Sometimes God does not answer our prayers but expects us to answer them for ourselves. Once I asked God to have compassion on an old man I saw at a distance carrying two large sacks of groceries. God said, "You have compassion on him."

Many unsaved people who encounter problems in their life don't hesitate to pray and cry out to Jesus to intercede, but you know, God doesn't hear their prayers. He is not obligated to because they are not His children.

I will make mention of the so-called "sinner's prayer", an asking type of prayer whereby we ask God to do this and do that. It is not scriptural to ask God for salvation; we confess to God the Father our "belief" in what His Son, Jesus, has already accomplished on the Cross.

Chapter 22

THE RAPTURE

Romans 8:11 "But if the Spirit of him that raised up Jesus from the dead dwell in you, he that raised up Christ from the dead shall also quicken your mortal bodies by his Spirit that dwelleth in you."

In other words, if we are saved, God, by His Holy Spirit that indwells us will change our mortal bodies to immortal bodies at the Rapture.

Romans 5:9 "Much more then, being now justified by his blood, we shall be saved from wrath through him."

Titus 2:13 "Looking for that blessed hope, and the glorious appearing of the great God and our Saviour Jesus Christ."

After the Crucifixion of Christ, God set Israel aside, and called the Apostle Paul to preach the Gospel of Grace, Christ and Him Crucified, to the world, predominately Gentiles, to call out a people for his Name.

This period of time which is referred to as the Age of Grace began about 40 AD when believers, according to Paul's Gospel, were first called Christians at Antioch.

This period of time will last approximately 2000 years and will end when the last believer is added to the Body of Christ, also called "The Church", and the "Bride of Christ".

The end of this period will be evidenced by an event commonly called "The Rapture", at which time Jesus, Himself, will come in the clouds and those Christians who have been saved by Christ's works on the Cross; both those who have died and those who are alive physically, will be given incorruptible bodies, and will rise to meet Jesus in the air, and will be with Him forever.

I Thessalonians 5:4 "But ye, brethren, are not in darkness, that that day (day of the Lord at time of rapture) *should overtake you as a thief."*

I know that in Matthew, Jesus says no man knows the day or the hour when the Son of man cometh. But that doesn't mean we can't know within two days. Besides, it is going to happen in a twinkling of an eye around the globe and it could be one day in some places and another day in other places.

I Corinthians 6:14 "And God hath both raised up the Lord, and will also raise up us by his own power."

Philippians 3:20,21 "For our conversation is in heaven: from whence also we look for the Saviour, the Lord Jesus Christ: Who shall change our vile body, that it may be fashioned like unto his glorious body, according to the working whereby he is able even to subdue all things unto himself."

II Corinthians 4:14 "Knowing that He which raised up the Lord Jesus shall raise us up also by Jesus, and shall present us with you."

Since we have been buried with Jesus, we also have been raised into new life, waiting for the adoption, to wit, the redemption of our body.

Other scriptures referring to the Rapture are (I Corinthians 15:52), (I Thessalonians 1:10; 4:13-18; & 5:9,10), and (II Thessalonians 2:1-3).

I know some of these scriptures may be hard for you to grasp, but really it's pretty simple; just get saved, live your life pleasing to God; wait for the trump to sound; and we're out of here. Hallelujah!

Chapter 23

HEALING

Healings wrought by the Apostle Paul:

Acts 14:8 ***"And there was a certain man at Lystra, impotent in his feet being a cripple from his mother's womb, who never had walked:"*** Paul, perceiving he had faith to be healed, said, "stand upon thy feet." And he leaped and walked.

Acts 16:16-18 Paul commanded a spirit of divination to come out of a damsel in the name of Jesus Christ and he came out the same hour.

Acts 19:11,12 God wrought special miracles by anointing handkerchiefs or aprons by the hands of Paul and diseases departed from the sick and evil spirits went out of them.

Acts 20:9-12 Paul raised a man from the dead. He had fallen down from the third loft.

Acts 28:8 Publius was the chief man of the island where Paul was shipwrecked. Publius' father lay sick with a fever and a body flux. Paul entered in, and prayed, and laid his hands on him, and healed him.

Acts 28:9 *"So when this was done, others also, which had diseases in the island, came, and were healed."*

Healing power of the Holy Spirit went out of Paul into the handkerchiefs and aprons. This power did not dissipate in the transfer of the cloths from Paul to the recipient. If Paul had the power to heal sicknesses and diseases, to raise the dead, and to cast out demons; then we who are believers, also have the power to do likewise, because the same Holy Spirit that indwelt Paul indwells us.

Now, here are some more scriptures concerning healing:

Isaiah 53:5 *"But he was wounded for our transgressions, he was bruised for our iniquities: the chastisement of our peace was upon him; and with his stripes we are healed."*

I Peter 2:24 *"Who his own self bare our sin in his own body on the tree, that we, being dead to sins, should live unto righteousness: by whose stripes ye were healed."*

Chapter 24

GIVING

II Corinthians 9:7 "Every man according as he purposeth in his heart, so let him give; not grudgingly, or of necessity: for God loveth a cheerful giver."

First off, if you don't give cheerfully, you may as well save time and money, and just keep it. Don't let someone or some organization or ministry coerce or compel you into buying something that doesn't amount to a hill of beans, or giving by promising you some outrageous return. We don't need that stuff being peddled on television. Jesus said It is finished. What He accomplished for us on the Cross, and the Word of God are all we'll ever need. If we will just be sensitive to the Holy Spirit, Who indwells us, He will tell us whom to give to, when to give, what to give and how much.

I don't believe you necessarily reap what you sow, like money for money, corn for corn, etc. We sow out of our plenty; we reap out of our need. I support one ministry and when the Holy Spirit lays it on my heart, I can't wait to put the check in he mail. Also, I ask the Lord, if He proposes to give me a reward, or a harvest; to give it to my son and his family in the form of good health, enough finances, to rebuke the devourer for their sake, and draw them nearer to Him. Hallelujah! And He does.

II Corinthians 9:6 "But this, I say, He which soweth sparingly shall reap also sparingly; and he which soweth bountifully shall reap also bountifully."

II Corinthians 9:8-10 "And God is able to make all grace abound toward you, that ye, always having all sufficiency in all things, may abound to every good work: (As it is written, He hath dispersed abroad; he hath given to the poor; his righteousness remaineth forever. Now he that ministereth seed to the sower both minister bread for your food, and multiply your seed sown, and increase the fruits of your righteousness;)"

Acts 20:35b "...ye ought to support the weak, and to remember the words of the Lord Jesus, how he said, It is more blessed to give than to receive."

Romans 12:20 says If thine enemy hunger, feed him, if he thirst, give him drink.

II Corinthians 8:12 Paul says "If you have a willing mind to give, give according to that you have and not according to that which you don't have." I would say that rules out pledges and faith promises.

Paul encouraged the Corinthians to be liberal in their giving, not as a commandment, but to prove the sincerity of their love. Our giving causes God to enrich our lives in everything to all bounti-fulness which causes us to give thanks to God. Our giving not only supplies the needs of others, but it causes them to glorify God and to long for the Grace of God which we have in ourselves.

Proverbs 19:17 "He that hath pity upon the poor lendeth unto the Lord, and that which he hath given, will he pay him again."

Proverbs 21:13 "Whoso stoppeth his ears at the cry of the poor, he also shall cry himself, but shall not be heard."

Proverbs 22:16 "He that oppresseth the poor to increase his riches, shall surely come to want."

Proverbs 28:27 "He that giveth unto the poor shall not lack; but he that hideth his eyes shall have many a curse."

I would say the Lord is very much interested in our helping and having compassion on the poor and the weak.

Lastly, God gave His best, His only begotten Son, to die on the Cross, so you and I could have eternal life. That's GIVING! That's LOVE!

Chapter 25

FORGIVENESS

Colossians 3:13 "Forebearing one another and forgiving one another, if any may have a quarrel against any: even as Christ forgave you, so also do ye."

Ephesians 4:32 "And be ye kind one to another, tender-hearted, forgiving one another, even as God for Christ's sake hath forgiven you."

After salvation, we forgive others because God has forgiven us (our sins).

There is nothing stipulated in Paul's Gospel, nor his writings that first we have to forgive everybody before we can be forgiven, like the Lord Jesus said during His earthly ministry. The Lord's Prayer isn't appropriate for us today. The Lord's Prayer was under Law. It was to Israel. It says, "Forgive others, that your Father which is in Heaven may forgive you." Under Law, absolutely, a Jew could not be forgiven until he forgave his neighbor. Jesus taught this in Luke 6:37, Mark 11:26 and Matthew 6:15. But today we're forgiven by the Grace of God. And Law and Grace don't mix.

I'm not speaking ill against forgiveness. I'm just pointing out some of the differences between Matthew's, Mark's, Luke's, and even Jesus' teachings and those which Paul taught. They must have been preaching a different gospel from Paul's gospel, the one by which we are saved today.

Chapter 26

THE LORD'S SUPPER

Jesus instituted the Lord's Supper at the Last Supper, at the Passover.

Matthew 26:20 "Now when the even was come, He sat down with the twelve."

Matthew 26:26,27 "And as they were eating, Jesus took bread, and blessed it, and brake it, and gave it to the disciples, and said. 'Take eat, this is my body.' And He took the cup, and gave thanks, and gave it to them saying 'Drink ye all of it.'"

The disciples didn't have the foggiest notion of what all of this stood for. Jesus didn't explain it; it wasn't time yet. When we come to the writings of the Apostle Paul, in *I Corinthians, Chapter 11,* we understand what it was all for. The Lord's Table of the bread and the cup is a memorial of His death and what He accomplished on the Cross. On the night of the Last Supper, His death hadn't taken place yet.

I Corinthians 11:23-26 *"For I have received of the Lord that which also I delivered unto you, That the Lord Jesus, the same night in which He was betrayed took bread: And when He had given thanks, He brake it, and said, Take eat: this is my body, which is broken for you: this do in remembrance of me. After the same manner also he took the cup, when he had supped, saying, This cup is the new testament in my blood; this do ye, as oft as ye drink it, in remembrance of me. For as often as ye eat this bread, and drink this cup, ye do shew the Lord's death till he come."*

Partaking of the Lord's Supper is remembering what Christ accomplished on the Cross.

I Corinthians 11:27-30 *"Wherefore whosoever shall eat this bread, and drink this cup of the Lord, unworthily, shall be guilty of the body and blood of the Lord. But let a man examine himself, and so let him eat of that bread, and drink of that cup. For he that eateth and drinketh unworthily, eateth and drinketh damnation to himself, not discerning the Lord's body. For this cause many are weak and sickly among you, and many sleep."*

If, when we partake of the bread and the cup; and remembrance of what Jesus accomplished for us on the Cross does not excite our hearts anew and cause us to give honor and glory and blessing to Him in thanksgiving and praise, then we have partaken unworthily, are guilty of Christ's death, we damn ourselves to Hell, and are sickly and die. In reality, we are not saved. We are commemorating a work that hasn't taken place in our soul and spirit.

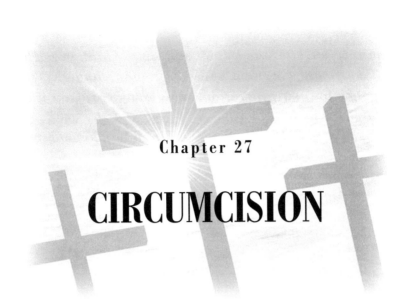

Chapter 27

CIRCUMCISION

About 2000 BC, God told Abram (later Abraham) to leave his country and go into a land He would show him and He would make of him a great Nation.

Genesis 13:16 "And I will make thy seed as the dust of the earth: so that if a man can number the dust of the earth, then shall thy seed also be numbered."

This is Abraham's earthly or fleshly family.

That was the beginning of the Jewish Nation, one special little race of people, God's chosen race, later called Israel. They were Covenant people.

Genesis 17:8 "And I will give thee, and to thy seed after thee, the land wherein thou are a stranger, all the land of Canaan, for an everlasting possession; and I will be their God."

Genesis 17:9,10 "And God said unto Abraham. 'Thou shalt keep my covenant therefore, thou, and thy seed after thee in their generation. This is my covenant which ye shall keep, between me and you and thy seed after thee; Every man child among you shall be circumcised:'"

This was a token whereby the seed of Abraham subscribed to the Covenant God made to Abraham and his seed. From then on, every man child of Abraham's generation was to be circumcised at the age of eight days.

Now, let's look at Abraham's Spiritual family:

Genesis 15:5 "And he brought him (Abram) *abroad, and said, 'Look now toward heaven, and tell the stars, if thou be able to number them: and he said unto him, So shall thy seed be.'"*

This is Abraham's heavenly or spiritual family; us.

Genesis 15:6 "And he believed in the LORD: and he counted it to him for righteousness."

We are made righteous today by believing on Christ and Him Crucified.

All through the Old Testament and up to Jesus dying on the Cross, God dwelt primarily with the Jew through covenants of promise, prophets, and the Law as given to Moses.

Ephesians 2:11b "...who are called Uncircumcision by that which is called the Circumcision in the flesh made by hands;"

The Uncircumcision was the Jewish term for a non-Jew. Sometimes they would add the word "dogs". "Uncircumcised dogs" is what they thought of Gentiles.

Ephesians 2:12 *"That at that time* (while God was dealing with the circumcision, Israel) *ye* (uncircumcision, Gentiles) *were without Christ, being aliens from the commonwealth of Israel and strangers from the covenants of promise, having no hope, and without God in the world:"*

That was the lot of the Gentile world, because God was dealing with Israel. But the day came when Israel rejected everything and God turned to the Gentile world through the apostle Paul.

Colossians 2:13 *"And you, being dead in your sins* (a spiritual death) *and the uncircumcision of your flesh,* (that's where we were genetically. We're not in the earthly family of Abraham, but rather we were Gentiles) *hath he* (God) *quickened* (or made us alive) *together with him,* (which of course ties us to His death, burial, and resurrection. And the moment we believed that Gospel of Salvation, God Forgave us) *having forgiven you all trespasses;"*

Colossians 2:11 *"In whom* (Christ Who is the fulness of the Godhead bodily) *also ye are circumcised* (now we are circumcised, not in the flesh, but Spiritually) *with the circumcision made without hands, in putting off the body of the sins of the flesh* (remember circumcision depicts a cutting off of that which was superfluous. So for the believer, now we have had something cut off which is no longer necessary and it is the Old Adam) *by the circumcision of* (or by) *Christ:"*

Physical circumcision for us today is not mentioned in the Bible. Whether it is or is not a good thing from a sanitary standpoint, or any other reason, should be discussed with your doctor.

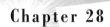

Chapter 28

REASONS FOR ASSEMBLING WITH OTHER BELIEVERS – LOCAL CHURCH

1. Hear and study the Word.

    a. For the perfecting (maturing) of the saints.

    b. For the edifying (building up) of the Body of Christ.

    c. For the work of the ministry.

2. To become more adept at soul winning.

3. To pray for one another.

4. To learn more about our Lord and Saviour, Jesus Christ; to gain knowledge of the Scripture.

Ephesians 4:12 "For the perfecting of the saints, for the work of the ministry, for the edifying of the body of Christ:"

These are the criteria for any local group of believers. That they mature in Christ, that they may be built up. strengthened, and that they might know that by which they are saved. That they might grow in their ability to lead others to salvation.

Romans 7:4 *"Wherefore, my brethren, ye also are become dead to the law by the body of Christ* (that is His crucified physical body)*; that ye should be married to another, even to him who is raised from the dead, that we should bring forth fruit unto God."*

In a physical marriage God expects the fruit of that marriage to be children; so also, God expects the fruit of the believer should be other believers, and we call that soul-winning.

II Corinthians 5:20a *"Now then we are ambassadors for Christ,..."*

First, we must realize, after salvation, our citizenship is in heaven. We are in this world, but not of it. An ambassador is a representative of his home country; in our case, heaven, living in a foreign country; in our case, the world. We have been appointed ambassadors by God to tell (witness to) the world about all the benefits our world and our Lord and Saviour, Jesus Christ, have to offer, most importantly salvation and eternal life. So we will want to search the scriptures to show ourselves approved, rightly dividing the Word of Truth. I might add, ambassadors don't have to worry one whit about their needs. Our Lord Jesus provides it all in abundance.

Even though salvation is an instantaneous, one-time event, Christian growth and Bible understanding are continuing processes. And what better way to grow in these than to fellowship regularly with those of like kindred; believers.

Note that two of the three scriptures referred to, involve witnessing to the lost. I would say that one-on-one witnessing should be the number one priority in a Christian's life.

Chapter 29

NO EXCUSE –
FOR NOT BEING SAVED

Some might say that some have never heard the Gospel or have never had a chance to accept Christ as Saviour. Let's see what the scriptures say:

Romans 1:18-20 *"For the wrath of God is revealed from heaven against all ungodliness and unrighteousness of men, who hold the truth in unrighteousness: Because that which may be known of God is manifest in them, for God hath shewed it unto them. For the invisible things of him from the creation of the world are clearly seen, being understood by the things that are made, even his eternal power and Godhead; so that they are without excuse."*

Titus 2:11,12 *"For the grace of God that bringeth salvation hath appeared to all men, Teaching us that, denying ungodliness and worldly lusts, we should live soberly, righteously, and godly, in this present world;"*

John 1:6 *"There was a man sent from God, whose name was John* (the Baptist).*"*

John 1:7 *"The same came for a witness, to bear witness of the Light, that all men through him might believe."*

John 2:9 *"That was the true Light, which lighteth every man that cometh into the world."*

All men, past and future have received or will receive opportunity, somehow or other to accept the Light.

Romans 3:26b *"...that he* (the Lord Jesus) *might be just* (or fair),... *"*

You might ask, "How will God justify, sending someone to the eternal Lake of Fire when so far as we know they never had an opportunity to hear the Gospel? The only way we can answer this question is that everyone sentenced to the Lake of Fire will have had opportunity and has rejected the Light (the Saviour). God is never an unjust or unfair God.

If you cannot comprehend the above, consider the following:

I do not believe that all fetuses, babies, and children below the age of accountability will automatically go in the Rapture or otherwise be saved. It would not be fair (and God is fair) to others. I believe the names in the Lamb's Book of Life have been there from the foundation of the world and there is no changing them. I base this on the fact that God foreknows everything, and names are in the Book depending upon, not only how we choose, but how insane people would have chosen had they been sane, and how little ones would have chosen had they lived and had opportunity to choose. In other words, God sees their lives lived in His mind. But whatever you believe; remember, God is never unjust or unfair. All will have an opportunity to accept or reject Christ. There will be no excuses.

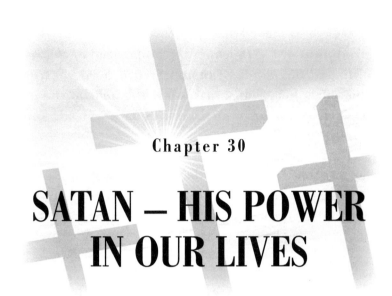

Chapter 30

SATAN – HIS POWER IN OUR LIVES

In the beginning when man was created, Satan beguiled (deceived) Eve into sinning and Adam followed suit and sin entered into the heart of man. Mankind fell out of fellowship with God. Adam had been given rule over the entire earth, but when he sinned, he lost that dominion and Satan took it and has been and now is the God of this world. God foreknew man would sin, and from the foundation of the world, had a plan to restore man into fellowship with Him (God). Ever since Adam sinned, Satan has been trying to thwart this plan of God. Satan tried by polluting the blood line through which Christ would come, by killing all the babies when Jesus was born in the flesh, and by putting in the minds of the chief priests of the Jews to have Jesus crucified, not knowing that "Jesus Crucified on the Cross" was in the plan of God. The Cross is our way (the only way) of salvation today, to bring us back into right standing with God.

II Corinthians 4:4 "*In whom the god* (Satan) *of this world hath blinded the minds of them which believe not* (tries to keep the sinner from getting saved) *lest the light of the glorious gospel of Christ, who is the image of God, should shine unto them.*"

But for the same unbelievers, the Holy Spirit of God not only convicts of sin, woos, and draws them, and gives them receptive hearts for salvation; but overrides Satan's blinding and gives the measure of faith to believe for salvation.

Proverbs 14:12 "*There is a way which seemeth right to a man but the end thereof are the ways of death.*"

Satan has also blinded us by causing us to be satisfied with our present religious status. Most of us think we are saved, but most have not even heard the True Gospel. We think we are saved because we accepted the only gospel that was ever presented to us, because we go to church two or three times a week, we fast periodically, do good works, pay tithes, are baptized in water, etc. And when we pray, being unbelievers, God does not hear us (is not obligated to answer) because we are not His children. But, Satan answers just enough of our "so-called" prayers to satisfy us and make us feel spiritual, and to keep us blinded to true salvation. We don't realize it, but the devil has us right where he wants us, thinking we're saved.

I Corinthians 10:13 "*There hath no temptation taken you but such as is common to man: but God is faithful, who will not suffer you to be tempted above that ye are able: but will with the temptation also make a way to escape, that ye may be able to bear it.*"

Satan tempts people to sin but cannot force people to sin. He tempted Jesus (Matthew 4:1-11) but Jesus defeated him with the Word of God. God will not permit Satan to put any more on the believer than that which he is able to bear.

***II Corinthians 11:13-15** "For such are false apostles, deceitful workers, transforming themselves into the apostles of Christ. And no marvel; for Satan himself is transformed into an angel of light. Therefore it is no great thing if his ministers also be transformed as the ministers of righteousness; whose end shall be according to their works."*

Paul was telling the Corinthian believers not to be deceived and not to allow their minds to be corrupted by false doctrine being preached by those who were being led by Satan, who had power to counterfeit the things of Christ.

Satan is also called the Devil. His army of servants are called demons. Satan is the prince of the power of the air (Ephesians 2:2). He is the accuser of the brethren (Revelation 12:10). He accuses the saints, day and night, before the throne of God, but God the Father sees us as righteous through the blood of His Son.

***I Peter 5:8** "Be sober, be vigilant; because your adversary, the Devil, as a roaring lion, walketh about, seeking whom he may devour:"*

John in Chapter 10, verse 10, says, "The thief (Satan) cometh not, but for to steal, and to kill, and to destroy." He also says in I John 4:4b "Greater is He (the Holy Spirit) that is in you (us) than he (Satan) that is in the world." We believers will never in this life be free from the oppression of the devil, but we have sufficient power through the Holy Spirit to overcome him.

If you stay in your present condition as a sinner, you will end up for eternity, with Satan in the lake of fire. If you believe and accept Jesus Christ as your Saviour and Lord, you will not only have abundant life here on earth, but you will have eternal life with Jesus.

Chapter 31

THE TRIBULATION

Daniel 9:24 *"Seventy weeks are determined upon thy people and upon thy holy city, to finish the transgression, and to make an end of sins, and to make reconciliation for iniquity, and to bring in everlasting righteousness, and to seal up the vision and prophecy, and to anoint the most Holy."*

A week is seven, so seventy weeks of years is 490 years. The King of Persia gave Nehemiah permission to rebuild Jerusalem and the Temple. From the date of the decree to rebuild, up until Palm Sunday, the rejection of the Messiah, was 483 years or 69 weeks. The 70th week or the final seven years is referred to as the Tribulation, which is future. And I might add – very near future. This seven years is primarily God dealing with the Nation of Israel; however, all the world will become involved.

During the Tribulation, the wrath of Satan and the wrath of God will be poured out on the earth.

Matthew 24:21 "For then shall be great tribulation, such as was not since the beginning of the world to this time, nor ever shall be."

Not even the plagues of Egypt will be close in comparison. At least two thirds of the Jews will be killed and probably a greater percentage of the rest of the world.

The Anti-christ will come out of the geographical area that comprises the ancient Roman empire and from the people, the Romans, who destroyed the Temple in 70 AD (Daniel 9:25,26). The Anti-christ will be a Jew (Daniel 11:37).

I don't want to go into a lot of detail about the Tribulation, but I do want to cover some things that pertain to us today.

First, The Church has just been given incorruptible bodies and raptured (taken out bodily from this world) to be eternally present with their Lord and Saviour, Jesus Christ. The Church Age will be over, having ended with the last member (believer of the Cross) being added to the Body of Christ. Secondly, Anti-christ has come on the scene as ruler of the world. The Jews will accept him as their Messiah. Israel is looking for their Messiah to come the first time, because they don't recognize that Jesus Christ was the Messiah.

John 5:43 "I am come in my Father's name, and ye receive me not; if another come in his own name, him you will receive."

Anti-christ will allow the Nation of Israel to resume their Temple worship, with their animal sacrifices, and other Law-related rituals as when Jesus walked the earth. Instead of salvation by the Gospel of Grace, salvation will revert to the Gospel of the Kingdom as it was being proclaimed at the time of Christ and Peter and the eleven (Matthew 24:14).

Thirdly, **Matthew 24:14** *"And this gospel of the kingdom shall be preached in all the world for a witness unto all nations; and then shall the end come."* I know just about everybody today believes the rapture cannot occur without the fulfillment of this scripture; but it is talking about another gospel and one which the 144,000 Jewish men, 12,000 from each tribe of Israel, will preach to the whole world during the Tribulation period.

Lastly, some people reject salvation today, thinking that they will get saved later on, or, even as a last resort, during the Tribulation. But, scripture states that those who have heard The Gospel, and rejected it, will NOT have a second chance during the Tribulation.

II Thessalonians 2:10-12 *"And with all deceivableness of unrighteousness in them that perish; because they received not the love of the truth, that they might be saved. And for this cause God shall send them strong delusion, that they should believe a lie: That they all might be damned who believe not the truth, but had pleasure in unrighteousness."*

Now we need to explain some things. Those who will be ready to accept the coming of the Anti-christ will be those who have heard the Gospel, the truth of the Word of God, but they loved their unrighteousness and they spurned God's offer of salvation. God is going to send these unbelievers "strong delusion" to believe the "lie" of Satan, that the Anti-christ is the God of this world, the one they have been looking for.

Paul, in **Ephesians 1:13,** states that *"the word of truth" is "the gospel of your salvation."* Also, in *I Corinthians 15:1-4,* Paul tells us what *"The Gospel" is: That Christ died on the Cross, shed His blood for our sins, was buried, and rose from the dead.* When you believe, beyond a shadow of a doubt, with all of your heart, that Christ did all these things just for you, God saves you and accounts your faith unto you as righteousness.

Many people have never heard "the Gospel", mainly because no one ever preached "The True Gospel" to them, so they will have an opportunity to be saved during the Tribulation. More than likely they will be killed for their stand for Christ. But, you are reading this book and you are hearing "The Gospel". Believe it, receive it, and live for God the rest of your life or until the Rapture occurs. You won't have to worry about the Tribulation, the Lake of Fire, or have anything to do with either. You will have life eternal in Jesus Christ. Hallelujah!

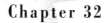

Chapter 32

HOW TO WITNESS

Romans 7:4 "Wherefore, my brethren, ye also are become dead to the law by the body of Christ, (that is His Crucified Physical Body) *that ye should be married to another, even to him who is raised from the dead, that we should bring forth fruit unto God."*

In a physical marriage God expects the fruit of that marriage to be children; so also, God expects the fruit of the believer should be other believers, and we call that soul-winning. After you become a believer, you will want to go into the entire world and tell everyone how they can become saved. The Holy Spirit will give you a boldness, power, and a desire to witness to others. Soul-winning should be the top priority and primary mission of every Christian. Solomon assured us that "he who wins souls is wise". (Proverbs 11:30).

A good outline for witnessing is as follows:

   1. Show them their need for a Saviour.

    a. ***Romans 3:23*** *"For all have sinned and come short of the glory of God;"*

    b. ***Romans 6:23a*** *"For the wages of sin is death;..."*

2. Tell them that God has paid the penalty for sin.

    a. ***Romans 5:8*** *"But God commendeth his love toward us, in that, while we were yet sinners, Christ died for us."*

    b. ***Romans 6:23b*** *"...but the gift of God is eternal life through Jesus Christ our Lord."*

3. Tell them how to receive this forgiveness for sin and to be saved.

    a. Paul's Gospel.

    b. "Salvation Prayer" at the end of Chapter "How We Are Saved Today".

    Explain each item of the Prayer and tell them that the salvation Jesus Christ provided on the Cross is a free gift, and all they have to do to receive it is to believe; really believe.

When witnessing, your opening remarks should be casual and of a subject of their interest. Later, you can divert the conversation to spiritual matters. Some examples of remarks you may use are:

Do you believe in Hell?

Do you believe in Heaven?

What happens to a person when he dies?

If you were to die right now, are you ready to meet God?

Do you ever give much thought to spiritual things?

Have you ever really thought about becoming a Christian?

If you were to die today, on what basis do you think God should let you into Heaven?

You will generally know how to proceed by the answers they give you.

I Corinthians 1:18a "For the preaching of the Cross is to them that perish foolishness:..."

I Corinthians 2:14 "But the natural man (the unbeliever) *receiveth not the things of the Spirit of God; for they are foolishness unto him; neither can he know them, because they are spiritually discerned."*

Sometimes, when you are witnessing to people, they might quote a scripture they think they know something about. Don't argue with them; just show them the previous two scriptures. If they say they are saved, ask them how they became saved.

II Corinthians 4:3,4 "But if our gospel be hid, it is hid to them that are lost: In Whom the god of this world (Satan) *hath blinded the minds of them which believe not, lest the light of the glorious gospel of Christ, who is the image of God, should shine unto them."*

Romans 3:11 No man seeks after God.

Before you approach someone to witness to, first say a little prayer asking the Holy Spirit to anoint you with His power and to give you a boldness and the words to say. Also, before asking a person to accept Jesus and what He did on the Cross, ask to have a word of prayer. In this prayer, bind the satanic force in the person's mind and ask the Holy Spirit to give the individual a clear mind and a heart receptive to the Gospel.

If the person gets saved, encourage him to find someone of like kindred to fellowship and study the Word with. It might be you.

I believe personal witnessing is the way God intends for His Salvation to be spread throughout the world; one-on-one.

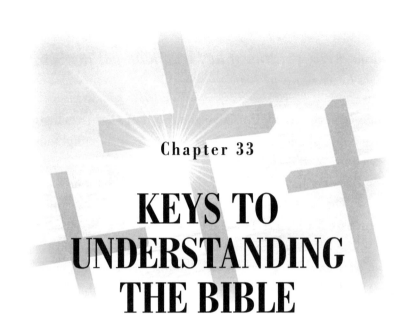

Chapter 33

KEYS TO UNDERSTANDING THE BIBLE

I Corinthians 1:18 *"For the preaching of the Cross is to them that perish foolishness* (not understood)*; but to us which are saved, it is the power of God."*

I Corinthians 2:14 *"But the natural man receiveth not the things of the Spirit of God: for they are foolishness unto him: Neither can he know them, because they are spiritually discerned."*

I Corinthians 6:19,20 *"What? know ye not that your body is the temple of the Holy Ghost which is in you, which ye have of God, and ye are not your own? For ye are bought with a price: therefore glorify God in your body, and in your spirit, which are God's."*

Romans 8:9b "...Now if any man hath not the Spirit of Christ, he is none of his."

The above scriptures tell us that the Word of God is foolishness (not understandable) to the unsaved person. It is enlightened to the believer by the Holy Spirit who indwells him. The unsaved person does not have the Holy Spirit, no matter what he has been taught. The Holy Spirit indwells him immediately upon his believing what Christ did on the Cross. The Holy Spirit is everything to the believer (see Chapter "Works of the Holy Spirit") and one of His greatest works is enlightening His Word (which He wrote) to the believer. So, I would say, the first thing necessary for understanding the Bible is salvation.

Galatians 1:8,9 "But though we, or an angel from heaven, preach any other gospel unto you than that we have preached unto you, let him be accursed. As we said before, so say I now again, if any man preach any other gospel unto you than that ye have received, let him be accursed."

I think the vast majority of people today who profess to be Christians were supposedly saved by a false gospel as the Apostle Paul speaks of in the above verses. They really are so insecure in their so-called salvation experience that they don't act like Christians, but pretty much blend in with the rest of the world. They don't witness because they really don't know how. They don't study the Word because they can't understand it. They have been taught false doctrine so long, that they are steeped in it. In all probability, the true Gospel, the Gospel of Grace, Christ and Him Crucified, has not been preached to them. Be careful whom you listen to.

Miles Coverdale said, "It shall greatly help thee to understand scripture, if thou mark not only what is spoken or written, but of whom, and unto whom, with what words, at what time, in what place, to what extent, with what circumstances, considering what goeth before, and what followeth after.."

Don't confuse Israel with The Church. The word "church" mentioned in the Gospels is not "The Church". "The Church" is "us" today; the ones who are saved by the Gospel of the Cross. We are also members of the "Body of Christ", of which Christ is the Head. We are also the "Bride of Christ".

Don't mix Grace and Law. Today, we are not under Law, but under Grace. When we mix Law and Grace, Satan smiles and God is grieved.

We are not under covenants. Covenants were directed only to the Nation of Israel. Now, in Christ Jesus, we are made nigh unto God, not by covenants, but by the Blood of the Lamb (Jesus).

Paul's writings to the Gentiles are the thirteen books of Romans through Philemon. This is the part of the Bible that a new believer should read and study first. Although Paul also wrote the Book of Hebrews, he wrote it to the Jewish believers who had been saved under the gospel of the kingdom, another gospel preached by the twelve apostles. "Hebrews" was not written to the gentiles. After getting firmly established with the above, we should study the entire Word of God because all scripture is by inspiration of the Holy Spirit, is profitable to us, and ties everything together.

All through human history, God has dealt with different people, in different ways. Today, we are not saved by rules, regulations, or by works; but only by believing on the Cross, and what Jesus did for us there.

***Ephesians 1:18a** "The eyes of your understanding being enlightened;..."*

***Romans 15:4** "For whatsoever things are written aforetime were written for our learning, that we through patience and comfort of the Scriptures might have hope."*

***II Timothy 3:16** "All scripture is given by inspiration of God, and is profitable for doctrine, for reproof, for correction, for instruction in righteousness:"*

Chapter 34

FROM NOW ON

The next major event in this world will be the "Rapture", the catching away of the Church, the saints of God. This could take place any time because there is nothing left, that has to happen before the Rapture – contrary to popular belief. I think the Rapture will involve so few people that it will hardly be noticed.

Now would be a good time to quote some scriptures and comment on happenings in the past concerning few people being saved:

When the earth was destroyed by water, there were only eight people saved: Noah, his wife, his three sons and their wives. Even though, after calling Noah into the Ark, God left the door open seven days, no one entered into salvation. One man made a calculated guess of how many people were on the earth then. About 1600 years from Adam to Noah – four to five billion people. Think of it – eight people saved out of that many.

When God destroyed Sodom and Gomorrah, only Lot and his two daughters were saved.

Matthew 22:14 "For many are called, but few are chosen."

Luke 13:24 "Strive to enter in at the straight gate; for many, I say unto you, will seek to enter in, and shall not be able."

Matthew 7:13,14 "Enter ye in at the strait gate; for wide is the gate, and broad is the way, that leadeth to destruction, and many there be which go in thereat: Because strait is the gate, and narrow is the way, which leadeth unto life, and few there be that find it."

Matthew 7:21-23 Not everyone who calls Jesus Lord, or who has prophesied or who has cast out devils, or who has done many wonderful works in His name, will be saved. The Lord will say to them, I never knew you: depart from me, ye that work iniquity.

Immediately following the Rapture, the seven-year Tribulation will take place. Even though this period of time is directed to the Nation of Israel, the whole world will be involved. The great majority of the people of this world will be killed during this period.

Then following, will be the 1000-year Kingdom (Millennium), in which Jesus Christ will reign as King of Kings and Lord of Lords.

At the end of the Millennium, all non-believers, past and present, will be judged (Great White Throne Judgment), sentenced, and cast into the Lake of Fire.

Then a New Heaven and a New Earth – *Revelation 21:1 "And I saw a new heaven and a new earth; for the first heaven and the first earth were passed away; and there was no more sea.*"

See also **II Peter 3:10.**

The Great City, the New Jerusalem; a cube, 1500 miles in each direction. The nations surviving at the end of the 1000-year reign of Christ will slip into eternity, but will be on the new earth.

Chapter 35

DEFINITIONS

Following, are some definitions that may help you in your study of the Word.

admonish – warn

admonition – gentle reproof

affliction – continual suffering

apostasy – the turning away from the revealed truth of the Word of God

apostle – one sent forth

appropriate – to take for one's own use

atonement – the reconciliation between God and man

attribute – to consider as belonging to

beguiled – deceived

believe – to accept the truth, existence, worth, etc. of something

carnal – fleshly nature

chaste – pure in thought and in style

chasten – discipline by punishment or affliction

communion – fellowship

companion – comrade

confess – acknowledge

consecrated – set apart as sacred

disciple – one sent forth

edify – lift up

enmity – hostility in action

entreat – ask earnestly

estrangement – alienation

eternity – forever and ever and ever – no ending

exhort – encourage

faith – belief without evidence

falling away – departure

gazingstock – person gazed at curiously or scornfully

glorified – given highest honor

grace – unmerited love and favor of God in Christ

holiness – separated to God, set apart, by the Blood

image – likeness

imputed – counted; reckoned

infirmities – physical, mental, or moral weaknesses

iniquities – wrongful, unjust acts

inspiration – God-breathed

justification – to declare one righteous (God declares a person just on the basis of acceptance of the shed blood of Christ)

mediator – one who settles disputes between parties

mercy – act of treating us with less severity than we deserve

mortify – to subdue or discipline; put to death

nigh – being close by; closely allied in kinship

offence – any sin, wrong, or fault

perdition – eternal death

physical death – separation of the soul and spirit from the physical body

preincarnate – embodied in human form

priest – go between; between God and man

profess – acknowledge

prophet – one who speaks for God

propitiation – the satisfaction (the shed blood) of the just demands of God's holiness for the punishment of sin

quickened – returned to life; revived; made alive

ransom – price paid

rebuke – strong expression of disapproval

reconciliation – the restoration of man to fellowship with God

redeemed – bought with a price; brought back from being lost

redemption – a ransom; the price paid to free a slave; to be bought; to deliver by paying a price

religion – man's attempt to reach God

righteous – upright; virtuous

repent – to feel sorry for one's sins so as to change

reproach – disgrace

reprobate – hardened in sin and unbelief; condemned to damnation

reproof – rebuke

sacrifice – that necessary to bring God and man together

sacred – set apart to religious use

sanctify – set apart as holy

saved – delivered from spiritual death or the consequences of sin; redeemed

scourgeth – punish severely

sin – disobeying God

spiritual death (2nd) – separation from God for eternity

substitution – the death of Christ was substitutionary; in our place

succor – aid

supplicate – ask for humbly

tabernacle – portable sanctuary; temple; human body

theophany – a manifestation or appearance of a deity to man

transgression – overstepping the law

trespasses – voluntary transgression of law

allegory – prolonged metaphor

emblem – visible sign of an idea

metaphor – one thing is called another

parable – truth illustrated by a factual story

shadow – representation of things to come

simile – one thing is compared to another

symbol – a thing or act representing something spiritual

type – an object or event used to prefigure another object or event

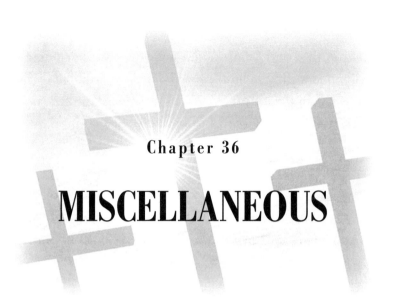

Chapter 36

MISCELLANEOUS

These are various scriptures or sayings that maybe didn't fit well with other chapters of this book; but are included for our learning and our living as Christians.

When Paul speaks of "faith in Christ", he's speaking of that whole finished work of redemption, which is faith in His death, His shed blood, His burial, and His resurrection.

Hebrews 9:12 *"Neither by the blood of goats and calves, but by His* (Jesus') *own blood, He entered in once into the holy place* (in heaven) *having obtained eternal redemption for us,"*

Hebrews 10:12 *"But this man* (Jesus)*, after He had offered one sacrifice* (Himself) *for sins forever, sat down on the right hand of God;"*

Our "old lives" were nailed to the Cross with Jesus. By that we count ourselves DEAD to sin and ALIVE unto God.

We live in this world, but we are not of it. We have died with Christ to this world; we now live with Him on earth; but in "heavenly places" in the Spirit.

Covenants were directed only to the Nation of Israel. Now, in Christ Jesus, we are made nigh, not by covenants, but by the Blood of Christ. (Ephesians 2:13)

Luke 1:33 *"And he* (Jesus) *shall reign over the House of Jacob forever; and of his kingdom there shall be no end."*

Philippians 3:20 *"For our conversation* (whole tenor of one's life, acts, and thoughts) *is in heaven; from whence also we look for the Saviour, the Lord Jesus Christ."*

Philippians 4:13 *"I can do all things through Christ which strengtheneth me."*

Philippians 4:19 *"But my God shall supply all your need according to his riches in glory by Christ Jesus."*

I Timothy 2:5 *"For there is one God and one mediator between God and men, the man Christ Jesus;"*

I Corinthians 10:13 *"There hath no temptation taken you but such as is common to man: but God is faithful, who will not suffer you to be tempted above that ye are able; but will with the temptation also make a way to escape, that ye may be able to bear it."*

I Corinthians 12:31 *"no man can say that Jesus is the Lord, but by the Holy Ghost."*

Salvation is 100% by what Jesus did on the Cross.

The uncertainty of our salvation is because of a misunderstanding of what is required for salvation, attaining eternal life, and going to Heaven.

For whom the Lord loveth, He chasteneth.

II Timothy 3:5 *"In the last days, men shall have a form of godliness* (think they're saved), *but denying the power thereof: from such turn away."*

Mark 8:36 *"For what shall it profit a man, if he shall gain the whole world, and lose his own soul?"*

Romans 14:11 *"As I live, saith the Lord, every knee shall bow to me, and every tongue shall confess to God."*

Colossians 2:9 *"For in him* (that is, in Christ) *dwelleth all the fulness of the Godhead bodily."*

John 5:22 *"For the Father judgeth no man, but hath committed all judgment unto the Son."*

II Timothy 1:7 *"For God hath not given us the spirit of fear; but of power, and of love, and of a sound mind."*

Matthew 12:34b and Luke 6:45 *"...for out of the abundance of the heart, the mouth speaketh."*

Mark 7:15 *"It's not what goes into a man that defiles him, but that which comes out* (of the heart).

God, in time past spake unto the Jewish fathers by the prophets. God spake to the New Testament Jews by His Son when He (Jesus Christ) preached, taught, and healed on this earth for three years before the Cross. God continues speaking to us today by His Word and by His Holy Spirit.

God answers your prayers, not according to need, but according to your faith.

Sin unto death – when God determines that it is better for you to be dead than alive.

I Corinthians 8:2 "And if any man think that he knoweth anything, he knoweth nothing yet as he ought to know."

I Corinthians 8:6 "But to us there is but one God, the Father, of whom are all things, and we in Him, and one Lord Jesus Christ, by whom are all things, and we by Him."

I Corinthians 8:4 "We know that an idol is nothing in the world, and that there is none other God but one."

Romans 10:14,15a "How then shall they call on him in whom they have not believed? And how shall they believe in him of whom they have not heard? And how shall they hear without a preacher? And how shall they preach, except they be sent?" Friends, when be become Christians, we are sent to the lost.

When studying the Book of "Revelation", you need to study "Daniel", "Revelation", and Matthew, chapters 24 and 25 together. They fit together.

Now is the day of salvation.

I Timothy 6:17 Let not them who are rich in this world trust in their uncertain riches, but trust in the Living God, Who giveth us richly all things to enjoy.

II Peter 3:8 *"One day is with the Lord as a thousand years, and a thousand years as one day."*

Romans 12:9b *"Abhor that which is evil; cleave to that which is good."*

Romans 12:17 *"Recompense to no man evil for evil. Provide things honest in the sight of all men."*

Acts 23:8 *"For the Sadducees say that there is no resurrection, neither angel, nor spirit: but the Pharisees confess both."*

Mark 14:50 and Matthew 26:56 When Jesus was taken, His disciples all forsook Him and fled. Not one person appeared to take His part. Judas betrayed Him; Peter denied Him with oaths; and the other disciples forsook Him and fled.

Luke 19:37-40 A multitude of disciples praised God; Pharisees asked Jesus to rebuke them and Jesus said, if they should hold their peace, the stones would cry out.

John, Chapter 11 Could Lazarus who was dead four days, represent the Jewish Nation, who rejected God 4000 years and whom God at the end of the Tribulation raises from death?

I Timothy 2:4 *"It is God's will for all men to be saved, and come unto the knowledge of the truth."*

I Timothy 6:8 *"And having food and raiment let us be therewith content."*

Philippians 4:11b *"...I have learned, in whatsoever state I am, therefore to be content."*

Luke 13:24 *"Strive to enter in at the strait gate: for many, I say unto you, will seek to enter in, and shall not be able."*

Matthew 22:14 *"For many are called, but few are chosen."*

I Timothy 6:7 *"For we brought nothing into this world, and it is certain we can carry nothing out."*

I Timothy 6:10a *"For the love of money is the root of all evil:"*

Romans 14:12 *"So then, every one of us shall give account of himself to God."*

Colossians 3:2 *"Set your affection on things above, not on things on the earth."*

Colossians 3:23 *"And whatsoever ye do, do it heartily, as to the Lord, and not unto men;"*

I Thessalonians 5:16 *"Rejoice evermore."*

I Thessalonians 5:17 *"Pray without ceasing."*

I Thessalonians 5:18a *"In everything give thanks:..."*

I Thessalonians 5:22 *"Abstain from all appearance of evil."*

I Thessalonians 3:10b *"...if any would not work, neither should he eat."*

Ephesians 4:30a *"And grieve not the Holy Spirit of God."*

II Timothy 3:12 *"Yea, and all that will live godly in Christ Jesus shall suffer persecution."*

Romans 5:3,4 We glory in tribulation, knowing that tribulation worketh patience; and patience, experience; and experience, hope.

Love is that which seeks the other person's highest good.

When you mix Law and Grace, Satan smiles and God is grieved.

Romans 12:19 Avenge not yourselves; vengeance is mine; I will repay, saith the Lord.

II Corinthians 12:14b *"...The children ought not to lay up for the parents, but the parents for the children."*

Romans 8:9b *"...Now if any man have not the Spirit of Christ, he is none of His."*

Refilling or revival – no such thing.

Psalms 34:1 *"I will bless the Lord at all times: his praise shall continually be in my mouth."*

Psalms 34:19 *"Many are the afflictions of the righteous: but the LORD delivereth him out of them all."*

Psalms 53:1a *"The fool hath said in his heart, There is no God...."*

Psalms 53:3b *"...there is none that doeth good, no, not one."*

Psalms 103:12 *"As far as the east is from the west, so far hath he removed our transgressions from us."*

Proverbs 10:22 *"The blessing of the LORD, it maketh rich, and he addeth no sorrow with it."*

Proverbs 11:30b *"...he that winneth souls is wise."*

Proverbs 13:24 *"He that spareth his rod hateth his son: but he that loveth him chasteneth him betimes."*

Proverbs 14:12 *"There is a way that seemeth right unto a man, but the end thereof are the ways of death."*

Proverbs 21:9 and 25:24 *"It is better to dwell in a corner of the housetop, than with a brawling woman in a wide house."*

Proverbs 21:19 *"It is better to dwell in the wilderness, than with a contentious and an angry woman."*

Proverbs 27:15 "A continual dropping in a very rainy day and a contentious woman are alike."

Proverbs 22:6 "Train up a child in the way he should go: and when he is old, he will not depart from it."

Proverbs 22:15 "Foolishness is bound in the heart of a child; but the rod of correction shall drive it far from him."

Proverbs 29:15 "The rod and reproof give wisdom: but a child left to himself bringeth his mother to shame."

Proverbs 29:17 "Correct thy son, and he shall give thee rest; yea, he shall give delight unto thy soul."

Times of the Gentiles – Jerusalem under Gentile control – ends at the second coming.

Fulness of the Gentiles – when the last person has been added to the Body of Christ – will end at the Rapture.

Day of Christ – the Rapture.

The Day of the Lord, the Day of Jehovah, the Day of God – this period of time, including the Tribulation, and into the Second Coming, and the setting up of the Kingdom.

Body – external, visible part of man – five senses: sight, smell, hearing, taste, and feel.

Soul – emotions (mind, will), memory, affections, conscience, reason.

Spirit – that part of man which knows; the breath (Spirit of life). Faith, hope, worship, prayer, adoration, and reverence.

Notes

Notes

Notes

Notes

Notes

Notes